The Power of You!

by

Olive Strachan MBE

To my mum, Althea collaire (nee St. Rose), the woman I most admire. Because of your guidance, support and love, I am the woman I am today! To my dad, Augustine Collaire, from whom I inherited my entrepreneurial spirit and joie de vivre!

To my husband, Errol Strachan, I am privileged to have had you at my side for most of my life, through the good times and the bad. I appreciate your love, support and wisdom.

CONTENTS

INTRODUCTION

"Our deepest fear is not that we are inadequate. Our deepest fear is that we are powerful beyond measure. It is our light, not our darkness, that most frightens us. We ask ourselves, 'Who am I to be brilliant, gorgeous, talented, fabulous?' Actually, who are you not to be?"
Marianne Williamson

INTRODUCTION

It has taken me a long time to grow and develop into the woman I am today. I have spent a great deal of my life feeling like a square peg in a round hole, trying to fit in. My earliest memories are of my parents trying to curb my exuberance. These early experiences remained with me into adulthood, where I tried my best to be like everyone else rather than accept and celebrate who I am. It has taken many years for me to realise that it is okay to be me. The fact is that I am a Black female consultant who has been running a business for over 20 years.

The organizations who pay for my services inform me that they employ me because I am different, I bring something to the table that is refreshing; and in organizations where I am the correct fit, I have established relationships that span decades.

I have evolved over the years, honed my skills and grown; as the learning and development industry has changed, I have changed with it, finding a variety of methods to help organizations and individuals to achieve their full potential.

Over the years I have spoken at many conferences, been a panel member at discussions regarding female entrepreneurship and the challenges we face, as well as working with diversity and inclusion and how we can combat and overcome racism.

Recently I spoke at a housing association conference called 'Balance for Better', where I was the keynote speaker. Some of the key themes were: changing perceptions (unconscious bias), attracting female talent (at all levels of the business), career progression (training and guidance for women), and a women's development programme.

I used my story to highlight the key themes that we were addressing and shared the highs and lows of establishing and growing a business. I discussed "imposter syndrome", which is when we feel inadequate, despite being successful, and when feelings of self-doubt persist. We feel that one day we will be found out!

Many famous public figures have admitted that they often experience imposter syndrome. The response from the staff at this conference was so enthusiastic that during lunch I had a queue of women from varying ages come to speak to me. The main message was that my story had inspired them. One particular lady waited until I was nearly leaving to tell me that she had woken up that morning feeling really upset and down but listening to my story had given her hope! I left the venue on cloud nine, knowing that I had had a positive impact on other women, and that I had made them feel better about themselves. It gave me a great sense of emotional satisfaction.

A few months after this experience, I received a request to speak for the WIMIN (Women in Manchester Insurance Network) Committee, which is part of the Insurance Institute of Manchester. It was an all-female audience and the title of my speech was, "How to defeat imposter syndrome and realise your potential". Once again, I shared my story about when it had happened to me and how I dealt with it, giving examples of my journey as a businesswoman. I also had the opportunity during the question and answer session to listen to the stories of other people.

These two recent experiences made me pause and reflect on my professional life. Frequently, after delivering a speech, I would be approached by women asking me for a copy of my book so that they could reflect on the key messages I had covered, and I had to say, "Sorry, I haven't written a book!" However, the seeds were sown and I started to think about what I could write, and to make some notes.

At the beginning of March 2020, I was working with a group of international consultants in Curaçao and I mentioned that I was writing a book, though as yet I didn't have a title for it. After listening to my speech many titles were suggested but the one that resonated with me the most was "The Power of You", because I have learned over the years that you have to have the correct mindset, which is about the power within. If you feel powerful you can achieve!

When I returned from Curaçao the Covid-19 pandemic descended upon us and I was in lockdown. I had been putting together chapters for the book over a period of time so during those three months I sat down and finally wrote my book. The purpose of this book is to share my story and by so doing I hope that, by reading about my challenges and how I overcame them, it will help others to realise that they are not alone. I also see this book as a legacy for my children and grandchildren.

At the moment I am living my best life! I have travelled extensively and made many friends and contacts, and I have learned a lot about myself along the way. Working for myself developed my self-confidence and self-esteem; it has made me strong and resilient but has also given me a great deal of pleasure and satisfaction.

In this book I will share with you the story of how I opened my business in 1998 with my credit card, and then in February 2019 visited Buckingham Palace to receive the MBE from Prince Charles, something that I never expected to happen to me. That is why it is important to understand that we all have the power within us to achieve!

CHAPTER 1

DEVELOPING MY SKILLS

I have experienced a range of careers but the one I feel had the biggest impact on me was working in the recruitment industry. I was 22 years old with a baby daughter and my husband, Errol, and I did not have a lot of money. I contacted Brook Street Recruitment in Manchester and went for an interview, taking my six-month-old daughter with me as I had no babysitter. My daughter was passed from person to person for a cuddle whilst I completed all the paperwork. The manager, Jenny Hilditch, and I got on famously; I felt we had a natural connection. Three hours later I went home having given them my neighbour's telephone number, as these were the days before mobile phones and I didn't have my own home phone at that time. I had applied for temporary or permanent work in customer services or typing.

The following week my neighbour ran across to my house to let me know that the agency had called me. To my surprise they had called to offer me a job working in the agency with them. This was a turning point in my life. I took to the recruitment industry like a duck to water, absorbing all the key learning points of the week's training course where I was taught to sell, build customer relationships, financial management, and influencing and persuading skills.

I was employed in the recruitment industry for eleven years, working for Brook Street; Reed Employment; opening the first ADECCO branch on Deansgate in Manchester; Premier Employment and Blue Arrow. The recruitment industry in the 1980s was a highly competitive environment. My confidence grew as I achieved and exceeded my sales targets and started to earn commission. These eleven years in the recruitment industry, where I had dealt with a variety of businesses from SME's to large organizations, helped to build the foundations and prepare me for working for myself and opening my own business.

A typical day as a recruitment consultant consisted of interviewing potential candidates and, whilst they were sitting with me, I would complete some cold calls and warm calls to find them the job of their dreams. Our daily target was twenty warm calls and eighty cold calls; we would call potential clients from the Manchester Evening News business pages and the Yellow Pages. Often, if we lacked candidates, I would sit at my desk on King Street in Manchester and look through the window and if I saw a likely candidate I would run out of the door and approach them, asking how happy they were with their present job and persuading them to come in and look at the opportunities we had on our books. I used to run to work in the morning because I found the work so exciting. By the time I left the recruitment industry, I was working as a manager with a team of four with additional responsibility for coaching new managers from other branches.

The industry had changed over the years, the one-to-one contact I had enjoyed with candidates had changed to dealing with large contracts and mass interviewing, and the relationship between me and the client, which was traditionally with either Human Resources (HR) or a Director, had now changed to dealing with someone whose sole responsibility was recruiting for the business.

I also felt that with my knowledge of recruitment and developing others, I was now ready to climb the ladder to the next step in my own career, having trained other managers within my company who had gone on to senior roles. I spoke to my manager about promotion opportunities only to be informed that although my skills were good enough to be a manager within the agency, I would need a degree to be promoted to the next level, which I did not have.

I left school at 16 with 'O' Levels and then completed a BTEC Diploma in Business Studies at college. During my time at the agency I had observed other staff joining the organization after me, benefiting from my training and coaching and then being promoted above me. I felt some discontentment and decided it was time to change my career, but the words from my manager about not having a degree kept troubling me.

I decided to gain the qualifications necessary to make me more attractive to potential employers and ensure that I would be on a level playing field with others. I kept on working full time and enrolled on the Post Graduate Diploma in Human Resource Management at Salford University on a part time basis, two evenings per week.

My manager was not supportive; in fact she was often obstructive when I tried to leave on time, making me late for my course. As far as she was concerned, I had sufficient skills to do the job I was paid for. I was also a wife and mother of two young children, with all the challenges that entailed, whilst trying to hold down a demanding full-time job with sales targets to achieve, but I persevered and eventually completed my two-year course and graduated.

Apart from gaining my Post Graduate Diploma I made some lovely friends, a lot of whom I am still friends with twenty-four years later, we meet for birthdays whenever possible. Some of my colleagues from the course have used me for training and consultancy work. One person in particular is Gail Howarth, who has been extremely supportive. As her career in HR has developed, she has taken Olive Strachan Resources with her and Gail has used my services whilst working at Rathbone Group, The English Institute of Sport and most recently at Sports Information Services Ltd (SiSTV). This kind of loyal support is what I have built my business on.

CHAPTER 2

CHANGING CAREERS

I retained my full-time job in the recruitment industry whilst completing my studies, keeping my management skills up to date by coaching and mentoring my staff. Then, as fate would have it, whilst working at Blue Arrow an organization called Video Arts rang with a vacancy for an office manager to set up a brand-new resource centre in Salford. It was exactly what I was looking for!

Video Arts is a London-based organization which provides engaging video learning solutions to businesses to support their employees' professional development. It was co-founded by the actor John Cleese together with Sir Anthony Jay back in 1972. They saw the need for a learning solution that would shake up the formal classroom experience and they decided to use entertainment to capture the imagination of participants.

As soon as I read the job description I knew I wanted the job because working in the Learning and Development field was part of my future goal. My vision was coming together! I was studying Human Resource Management at university, an element of which included helping organizations with their employees' professional development requirements, and the Video Arts job was an aspect of this. I put myself forward for the job, I was successful, and I left the recruitment industry.

I am passionate about learning - not just my own, but developing others. I thoroughly enjoyed working for Video Arts because their values were similar to mine and when you honour your personal values work becomes effortless. I find that when I work in an environment which has different values from mine, work seems a lot harder.

It was at Video Arts that I first heard the phrase, "Laughter and Learning". I had attended many courses where I spent a lot of time tuning out, or sometimes even having a nap, because the trainer wasn't engaging, and this phrase was something I could connect to.

As manager of the Video Arts resource centre I had to recruit a team and sell training resources to organizations in Manchester and Liverpool. Clients would come into the resource centre and look at videos to support staff learning. These videos typically starred familiar faces such as John Cleese, Dawn French, James Bolam, to name a few. We also had a video from the chef Jamie Oliver when he was at the height of his popularity, taking us through how he trained fifteen disadvantaged youths to be chefs. The videos had typical business scenarios which involved either leadership, management, or customer services but put across in a humorous manner. I would often hear clients laughing out loud whilst reviewing them.

Video Arts had an amazing array of resources and my team and I had to watch the videos and learn the key messages in order to be able to help and advise organizations about what was right for them. This was a pleasure for me because the content for the videos was designed by experts in the field of leadership, management development, etc.

My role also involved helping organizations with their learning needs. At that time 'creating a learning organization' was one of the key mantras of most businesses, so this was an amazing time for learning suppliers like me. Often clients would call us to help them with their competency framework, or their training needs analysis. I would sit down with them and match the resources we could supply with their mission, vision, values etc. We would also run events for clients such as Astra Zeneca, Matalan and Salford University, at their own premises for "Learning at Workday".

I really enjoyed my work; it brought together most of my skills: dealing with clients, arranging events, advising on learning and development needs, discussing performance management and leadership issues. Every day I woke up feeling a sense of purpose and passion for what I was doing. I also built some great contacts with both national and international organizations.

On a personal level there were lots of benefits in working for Video Arts and it gave me great insight into the training needs of different organizations. Whilst working in recruitment, the majority of clients I worked with were in the private sector. Working with Video Arts gave me the opportunity to build my contacts in the public sector. My role also involved delivering presentations with audiences of up to 200 people, so I was able to hone my presentation skills. Video Arts believed in rewarding their employees and frequently held social events where the stars from the training videos would attend. At one of these events I had the pleasure of meeting and speaking to John Cleese and Dawn French.

I had a very embarrassing experience whilst working for Video Arts, something happened which taught me a lesson I'd never forget. There is a video about how to run an exhibition, if I remember correctly the title was 'How not to exhibit yourself'. One of the managers from another office had been asked to attend an exhibition at Birmingham NEC, to show the video to some exhibitors to help them, and subsequently to man the stand and answer any questions. Unfortunately, the manager couldn't attend the event and asked if I could go in his place. I didn't ask any in-depth questions, in my mind I thought I'd just put the video on, let them watch it, and then go over to the stand.

On the day, I left Manchester at 6am knowing it would take about two hours to get to Birmingham. I saw myself arriving early, getting acquainted with my stand, possibly mingling around with other exhibitors. As I hit the motorway there was a sign saying there had been an accident on the motorway and that there would be a two-hour delay. Still enough time to get there on time, or so I thought. After sitting in the car for nearly three hours, I arrived in time to jump onto a podium and introduce the video, quoting a few key facts that I had read from the brochure.

The lights went down, and the video played. When the video finished the lights came on and I looked around at a sea of approximately sixty people.

I was just about to say, "I hope you found that interesting and picked up some key points about how to get the best from your exhibition", and then invite them to come to my stand to learn more about the vast array of training resources Video Arts could offer, when suddenly a man stood up and said he had a question for me. I had not prepared for questions! I kept a fixed smile on my face and nodded encouragingly. He said, "Before you introduced the video you gave some figures regarding how effective exhibitions could be if handled correctly. Could you quantify and qualify those figures?" The truth was that I could not, because I had just read them out from the booklet. I hastily said that the figures had been compiled by some research commissioned by Video Arts and I could find out where the data came from if he gave me his details, but later I was told by a colleague that I looked like a rabbit caught in the headlights! It was an uncomfortable moment and I didn't feel that I had acquitted myself well. This was a lesson well learned for future events/meetings.

Prepare, prepare more, research your subject, and don't quote figures when you don't know where they came from. Ask for exact details about what the brief is. And if there is a possibility that you may be late, stay in a local hotel the night before.

One of the key lessons I discuss when coaching is the importance of learning from your mistakes. Here is a recent recommendation written by one of my clients on LinkedIn, Maura Jackson, multiple-award winning CEO of multiple-award winning *Backup North West*, which demonstrates how much I have put those early lessons learned into practice.

"Olive is a force of nature! We used her to run a staff away day and she was a resounding success. Well prepared, well delivered, and well received. She did her homework too and designed activities which met our exact requirements. We had a fulfilling day focusing on the future of the charity, but we also had a lot of fun! Thanks Olive!!"

In 1998 Video Arts decided to close the regional offices and centralise the business in London. I was offered a role in London but as my family was in Manchester this was not feasible for me, so I was made redundant. I had two children and a mortgage and my first thought was to find a job, but at that time the jobs advertised were all aimed at 25-35 year olds and as I was approaching 37, I felt old and unwanted, and my confidence was very low at this time.

One thing that did give me a boost was my graduation from Salford University when I gained my Post Graduate Diploma in Human Resource Management. Graduating with my classmates and throwing our caps in the air was so exhilarating, it gave me a huge sense of achievement.

In the meantime, I had been discussing my lack of job prospects with my husband, and my dream of working for myself, and so after a celebratory graduation meal on Deansgate, in Manchester, I went into some serviced offices and paid for six months' office space (plus deposit) on my credit card. As I paid, I remember my heart beating very fast, because I knew that moment was a culmination of my dreams and this was a momentous point in my life.

Prior to this point, I had twice attempted to open a business in partnership with others, but it never felt right. The first attempt was whilst I was working in recruitment. One of my clients was an HR Director for whom I had recruited many staff over an 18-month period, and we had become friends. I had confided in her my frustration at the lack of advancement within my role in recruitment and she shared with me that she was considering opening a business with a contact of hers who was involved in executive search and selection. I was very fond of her and knew that our ethics were the same and we would work together well, however, after meeting her contact, who didn't seem to like or respect me, I had some doubts.

During meetings where we were discussing setting up the business, which was to be an equal partnership, he spoke over me and put forward his opinion like it was a fait accompli.

I knew that on paper our partnership sounded good - an HR Director, a recruitment specialist and an executive search and selection consultant - but in practice I knew I could not work with this person, so on the day that we were to sign the papers that would establish our partnership, I pulled out.

The next opportunity I had to open a business was with another recruitment consultant. She was excellent, beloved by clients and candidates alike, her name was known in the recruitment industry and she was highly respected. Together we would have made a successful team. We had many late-night discussions regarding what type of employment agency we would open, location, staff, etc., but once again I had my doubts.

The question I asked myself was why did I want to work for myself? The main reason was because I wanted to be my own boss, do things my way, without having to consult anyone.

Going into partnership with someone else did not tick any of those boxes. Also, this person had been my mentor when I first started in the recruitment industry; our relationship was mentor and mentee. If we were opening a business together I wanted an equal relationship, not with someone to whom I would have to keep deferring, so in the end I said no, that I wasn't ready to start a business. I also knew that I was heartily sick of the recruitment industry and if I was going to open a business it would not be in recruitment.

CHAPTER 3

OPENING MY OWN BUSINESS

Four strands led me to open Olive Strachan Resources (OSR) training consultancy in July 1998. The first strand was the deep reflection on the type of business I wanted to open and why. During my time in recruitment I worked closely with HR professionals who seemed unhappy with the way HR was perceived both within organizations and externally. HR was viewed in a negative light, dealing with staff issues such as redundancy and performance. If there was a problem then HR would deal with it. But there was no appreciation for the benefit of having an efficient HR department. If things were going right, the senior managers would ask, "Why do we need an HR department?", and if things were going wrong the question would be, "What's the point of having an HR department if we are in such a mess?" It seemed like a difficult and thankless task in 1998 and I decided that although I wanted to work in HR, I would prefer to focus on learning and development.

Strand number two was that as part of my two-year, part-time course at Salford University, I had to prepare a presentation to deliver to my class. My presentation was about implementing the Investors in People award, which is a standard for people management, offering accreditation to organizations that adhere to the Investors in People standard. As I delivered my presentation and the audience became engaged with what I was saying, I held their attention and felt a moment of pure joy. I knew that this was something that I enjoyed doing and wanted to do more of.

Strand number three was working with Video Arts. I learned from business professionals how to impart an important message in the right way. I worked with all types of organizations from those that employed fifty staff to those that employed more than ten thousand staff, each one seeking to increase staff performance through learning and development.

Learning could be challenging but fun. I wanted to help others to grow and develop. That was my calling.

The fourth and final strand was my own experience. Whilst working in recruitment part of my remit was to mentor/coach and develop others. Staff that I had coached would often rise within the organization and be successful, so I was confident in my abilities to develop and coach others.

I knew I wanted to work in learning and development, there were contacts in Manchester that I could call upon to get work both from my recruitment days and whilst working for Video Arts, the next step was to find suitable offices. During my time working in Manchester I had mainly worked in the city centre, other than a brief period when the Video Arts office was based in Salford. I wrote a report to senior management putting forward a compelling argument as to why we should move to central Manchester, they agreed, and we relocated to offices not far from Piccadilly in the city centre.

For my own business I knew that in order to achieve success quickly I needed an office that potential clients could find easily and Deansgate, the main road running through the city centre, was my preference. I would be working alone so I realised I needed a serviced office so that I could have some support whilst my business grew.

The first office I saw was based near the Ramada Hotel and was ideal but just as I was about to pay the deposit, I was told they were closing down due to lack of business.

Disappointed, I decided to keep looking until I found the right office in the correct location. On the day that I graduated from Salford University I passed a notice for serviced offices available on Deansgate and saw it as a sign.

Olive Strachan Resources was born! Initially I wasn't sure what to call my business but my husband suggested that as I had been working in Manchester and environs for many years, and many HR professionals knew my name either through recruitment or the training resources industry, calling the business Olive Strachan Resources made sense.

I had my office on Deansgate, now I had to make some money! My family still needed some financial input from me so I needed to make this work, and I knew I couldn't do it alone. I started by completing a personal SWOT analysis on myself, to assess my strengths and weaknesses but also to understand the external opportunities and threats.

My strengths were that I had worked in recruitment for eleven years, working closely with organizations from SME's to large companies, and was well known in Manchester. Whilst working for Video Arts I had built strong relationships with managers, directors and HR professionals within many organizations throughout the country, some of which continued to contact me to discuss their training needs.

Weaknesses: accounts were not my strong suit and I knew that I would need support in this area, along with technology.

In terms of opportunities, I knew that Video Arts had independent resource centres which stocked and sold their resources, so I suggested that I be one of their resource centres.

After all, I knew their product extremely well, had proven that I could sell them, and I had the contacts. I had amassed a lot of experience so far and felt that this redundancy could prove to be an opportunity in itself.

The threat to my new business was that I was a Black woman venturing into an established field of predominantly white males.

I reflected on the type of resources that had been used on previous courses I had attended, and realised that organizations used games, videos, books, etc., so I researched the suppliers for these resources and contacted them as well, in order to maximise my potential sales.

I now had a well-stocked resource centre supplied by organizations such as Gower, The Industrial Society, Fenman, the BBC, together with Northgate business games, to name a few. I had my office, my resources, and my husband - who is a wizard with figures - agreed to do my accounts for me until I got on my feet, as he was also working full time.

I was confident in my ability to sell via both telesales and face to face. When I opened my business in 1998 the main method of communicating with other businesses was telesales, face to face selling, the newspapers, or the Yellow Pages telephone directory.

Working as a resource centre for Video Arts meant that I did have a list of clients that had used training resources before, which was my 'warm' database, but I also purchased a list of organizations with 50+ staff from the Chamber of Commerce and spent my first three months just sitting on the phone in my office making telesales calls. When I received some interest, I would arrange a face to face meeting and try to close the deal.

Having worked in recruitment I was used to rejection, so I had no problem hearing the word 'no' time and time again. Eventually I had some conversions (clients who said 'yes') and started to make some money.

I was proud of my resource centre, where we stocked up to 500 resources, from videos which cost over £1000 to purchase, to books and business games.

I had a room with wall to wall resources and a TV and video where clients could sit down with coffee and biscuits and view resources in comfort. Within a year or so I had made a name for myself and clients would regularly drop in or call to buy training resources.

CHAPTER 4

GETTING EXPOSURE

There is a travel agent I use called *Travel Counsellors* and at the bottom of each email it says in bold, "DON'T KEEP ME A SECRET – tell all of your family and friends about me as that is how I continue to grow my business!".

I realised that if I was to build a sustainable business it was vital that organizations knew about me and what I could offer to them, but my business was self-funded and I didn't have the financial resources to invest in advertising. At that time the Manchester Evening News was the key lens through which one could see into the business world; new organizations opening or closing, those which were expanding or restructuring, etc. During my years in recruitment we used this newspaper to contact potential clients and read it every evening to keep abreast of current events in the area. To have an article in the MEN would send out a clear message that I was open for business but again, I didn't have any money to pay for one. My only hope was to create sufficient interest in OSR so they would want to write about me!

I did some research and found out who was in charge of editorial for the business section, was able to get their phone number, and started a campaign of phone calls. In 1998 there weren't many Black female training consultants and I decided to use this unique selling point to my advantage. I called the paper approximately ten times, each time leaving a clear message as to why I was calling. Finally, on my eleventh call, I was told to stop calling - they were sending someone round to my office on Deansgate to interview me. To my delight my persistence had paid off and I was in the paper! It was a brilliant start and some of my clients called me to congratulate me on the article.

CHAPTER 5

HOW MY BUSINESS EVOLVED

I now had an office on Deansgate, an arterial road running through Manchester city centre. I'd chosen a serviced office so I always had someone to answer my phone, giving the appearance of me having staff when realistically it was just me. I'd had an article written about me in the Manchester Evening News, now I wanted to start building my business.

The learning and development industry has always been of interest to me but over my working life I had attended many training programmes that were well researched and factual, albeit not very enjoyable or engaging. The trainer's focus was often on getting information across, rather than the pleasure of the learning experience. My goal for my business was to offer clients engaging and impactful learning opportunities that had been well designed, with excellent content, but fun!

I understood that in order to accelerate growth and create some stability I would need to have some kind of relationship with a larger organization, but it was vital that this organization had similar values to my own. I believed in making learning fun and engaging and Video Arts also had the same ethos. I immersed myself in the Video Arts content, watching their videos at every opportunity, and truthfully it wasn't that difficult because I really enjoyed watching them. I learned from the content and enjoyed the humour in the way it was designed. That is probably why that, although I sold resources for other training suppliers, 90% of our sales were for Video Arts' training resources.

The Resource Centre was the main source of revenue for my company initially. Changing from being a Manager of a resource centre for Video Arts to opening my own resource centre was seamless because many of the large clients were happy that they could still access resources locally. This was before the days of viewing films online. The business was growing, and external factors were working in my favour.

Many organizations wanted to create what we call "a learning organization" - a company that facilitates the learning of its members and continuously transforms itself. The concept of the learning organization was coined through the research of the strategist Peter Senge, and his book, "The Fifth Discipline" brought him into the limelight and popularized the concept of the learning organization. Since its publication, more than a million copies have been sold and in 1997 Harvard Business Review identified it as one of the seminal management books of the past seventy-five years. This meant a lot of investment in learning, not just training courses but providing staff with the ability to access learning at work.

The majority of large organizations wanted to establish their own learning resource centre on site. Typically, this would be stocked with videos, books, simulations, games, journals and exercises. This was a great time to be a supplier of training resources. Depending on the size of the organization and their training budget I would receive orders of between £1000 and £50,000 and would be paid commission on each sale. As the only resource centre in Manchester, based conveniently in the City Centre with ample parking nearby, I was the obvious choice. My viewing room was comfortable, and tea, coffee and biscuits were readily available. I treated clients with the warm welcome you would receive if you came to my home.

Clients' requirements varied. Some were content to have a tour of the centre and then be left to view resources at their leisure, with me checking on them periodically to ensure they were happy, whilst some HR and training managers would come in with a list of issues they needed to cover and were seeking specific training resources that would get the message across, in which case I would sit with them and help them to match the best resources to fit their organizational culture. Gradually, as the trust built with clients, they would either ring me with a list of requirements and ask me to select resources on their behalf, or they would fax the results of their training needs analysis to me and ask me to match the resources, invoice them, and send them to their organization.

During the 1990s, if an organization didn't spend its annual training budget they would be allocated less the following year, therefore, I would get many phone calls with clients needing to spend their budget within a certain time scale. The resource centre was so successful that I was informed by one of the managers at Video Arts head office in London that my resource centre brought in 20% of their total UK revenue. Some of my clients were Shell UK, Astra Zeneca, Isle of Man Government, Yell, The Inland Revenue and The British Council, to name a few. However, all good things come to an end and many organizations started to centralise their purchasing through their head offices, which were normally in London. There was a big drive from buying videos to streaming films instead. The viewing figures for the resource centre went from thirty-five clients per week to two or three at the most.

Thankfully, I could see the writing on the wall, I had commissioned some research into the training market and realised that I had to put my efforts into consultancy and coaching.

Whilst the resource centre had this tremendous growth, which was extremely rewarding, I was not fulfilling my desire to develop others through my training and coaching. The resource centre was proving successful - I was selling resources - but I was not using my training or coaching skills. I started to have in-depth conversations with each client that came in to assess any other potential sales opportunities. And I started to cross-sell and up-sell; cross-selling is when you sell a different product to the same customer. If a client already uses me for training resources, why not use me to deliver the training as well? I am a qualified trainer and I know the product inside out.

Up-selling is when you try to increase the amount the client is spending with you, for example, I have delivered a one-day programme for you and the feedback was extremely positive, I hear you are putting together a four-day management development programme, would you consider using me for that as well? This was not always successful but my philosophy is "if you don't ask you don't get" - all they can say is "no"!

Alongside the resource centre, from day one I always tried to raise my clients' awareness of what I could offer; sometimes I was successful and sometimes not. The resource centre facilitated me building some long-term relationships with clients, some of which have lasted for over twenty years. These include Campanile Hotels; Joanne Craughwell, who was the HR Manager at the time, came into the resource centre in 1998 and although she later emigrated to New Zealand, I still have a strong relationship with the organization and have continued to work with them. My current contact is Mark Aldridge, Director of Operations, and Mark and I have worked together for over ten years on a variety of projects including coaching, designing and delivering training for his managers, and speaking at staff conferences.

Jane Hanson, latterly of Irwell Valley Housing, has used my services for over fourteen years. I will not name all my clients but from these early years of running the resource centre, OSR has made some valuable and loyal contacts that still use me today. These contacts are also friends and I am extremely grateful to all of them for their support.

The relationship which has had the biggest impact on my business is with the British Council. It began with Steve Topson and Lisa Mulvey walking into my resource centre; we got on famously and remain friends to this day! Gradually things developed from me selling training resources to them and progressed to delivering training for them nationally. Over the past twenty years, I have delivered programmes designed by the British Council and also designed bespoke programmes for them. Along the way I have made some long and cherished friendships. I have kept in touch with many of the delegates that I have trained via social media and on frequent occasions someone who I trained years ago will contact me to request that I work with either the senior leadership team or help to develop their staff. The British Council has been a big part of the OSR story.

Over the next ten years, from 1998 to 2008, my business grew. I moved offices from Deansgate to the Triangle in Manchester; I had two offices and four staff, including my daughter and son, working for my business and I employed an accountant and a marketing company. We delivered coaching, training and consultancy services and had a healthy turnover.

The "FISH! Philosophy

Video Arts became the sole distributor for Fish! services in the UK and Ireland. The Fish! Philosophy was created in 1997 by John Christensen. He visited Pike Place fish market in Seattle and was amazed by the way the fish sellers were having fun during their work. They also gave their customers a lot of attention, making their visit more enjoyable.

John Christensen noticed that there were four core practices everybody could implement in their work and life, and he named this the Fish! Philosophy:

1. Choose your attitude;
2. Be there;
3. Make their day;
4. Play – have fun at work!

The video that demonstrates the Fish! Philosophy is a little unconventional, because it is a film of the actual fish market with several men throwing fish at each other and encouraging their customers to join in. Some organizations loved it because it made you think differently; it's full of energy and passion, they could see how it might have an impact on people's attitudes and how it could link to their own organization's values. However, some organizations did not like the concept of having fun at work, it was anathema to them.

On balance I would say 60% of organizations wanted to embrace the Fish! Philosophy and create a version of it in their organization. For them, the old adage of "happy staff makes for a happy workplace" really did ring true!

Video Arts were looking for consultants who wanted to help sell the Fish! concept to a UK audience, and discussed it at a meeting in London for all the resource centres. I was a big fan of the Fish! Philosophy, so I volunteered to work on this project and the arrangement was that any enquires received would be passed on to me.

I would call the client as a Video Arts representative, meet with them to discuss their needs, and then together with Video Arts would submit a proposal, and design, deliver or facilitate a session or workshop, and I would receive a fee for my services. This proved to be lucrative because at the time many organizations wanted to incorporate the Fish! Philosophy into their working practices.

As part of the preparation for being a Fish! facilitator I was flown to Minneapolis to receive training from John Christensen and his team at their head office. Arriving on the first day with eleven other facilitators who were all international trainers was quite an experience. The Fish! colours are yellow, purple, blue, green and orange, and the offices, along with John Christensen himself, were a mix of all of them! I was amazed, when I looked at his feet, that even his trainers were a bright orange, he really believed in "living his brand"!

I was definitely out of my comfort zone during the Fish! training. Overall it was beneficial, but I was unable to join in with a couple of the activities and it serves to remind me about the appreciation of cultural differences. One evening we had "campfire conversations", where we had to share experiences in our life that had had a deep emotional impact on us. There was an envelope under your seat that you had to open, read the instructions and then share. As each person opened their envelope they would read it, take a deep breath, start to talk - and then start to cry.

I watched in dismay as one person after another literally burst into tears. It takes a lot to make me cry and I could feel the pressure as it was finally my turn. Unfortunately, I could not squeeze out a single tear. I just clearly and succinctly discussed a situation that I had found challenging. I felt so hard-hearted as they moved on to the next person, who obligingly sobbed!

On the last night we had a get-together to celebrate the end of the training and that we were now fully-fledged Fish! facilitators. I was looking forward to a relaxed evening chatting to my new contacts when I heard the question, "What is your talent?" Excuse me, what?!

It reminded me of the film, Miss Congeniality, when she is asked what her talent is at the beauty pageant and because she hadn't prepared one ends up filling wine glasses with water to play a tune. That was me! I had no "talent" and felt a complete failure as others took out violins, guitars and all types of musical instruments, sang songs or read prepared poems. Luckily, I was not the only person in this predicament, and we spent most of the night looking at each other, shrugging and smiling as another musical genius took to the floor. Fortunately there were enough people performing that I was able to shake my head when it came to my turn, and make up for it by applauding enthusiastically for everyone else!

Being involved in selling, designing and delivering the Fish! Philosophy gave my business a growth spurt and developed my presentation skills. Most of the contracts involved presenting at staff conferences. I spoke at DHL's staff conference with an audience of 500 people, entitled "Creating a winning culture"; Littlewoods Shop Direct on "Putting the customer first"; and GlaxoSmithKline flew me to St Helier, Jersey, to deliver "Maximising Teamwork".

I worked with Weight Watchers and Unilever and - the piece de resistance - a staff conference for Domino Pizzas called "Don't Dream It – Be It" for over 1,000 people!

I was extremely nervous when I had to deliver my session at the Domino Pizza event; I had to not only prepare my speech but work to overcome my nerves.

When I deliver, I like to look at my audience and connect with them, but it wasn't possible here, it was just a sea of faces. I worked hard on my mindset, kept repeating my positive affirmations and visualised a positive outcome. It worked, but it was one of the hardest things I have had to do.

The session was successful and, as with everything I do, I always take some time afterwards to reflect and evaluate how I could improve. By constantly challenging myself it allows me to grow and develop.

CHAPTER 6

PERSONAL CHALLENGES

I achieved a lot of success and my drive and determination to succeed kept me going, however, it was not all plain sailing and I often found myself suffering from "imposter syndrome". This is a psychological pattern in which one doubts one's accomplishments and has a persistent internalised fear of being exposed as a fraud.

When I opened my business in 1998 I was a Black woman in her late thirties, an HR/learning and development consultant in a field where most of the consultants were white, middle-aged men, so often when I arrived at networking events or meetings I was not quite what people expected. I felt like I was the only one, very much like Randi Zuckerberg who, after working at Facebook for twelve years, quit because of the company's failure to increase the number of women working in the technology sector. She said she was tired of being "the only one".

One of my contracts was working for a pest control company and I had to travel to Leeds to deliver a sales training programme. I arrived really early because I was so excited. I walked into the offices and the Director's personal assistant approached me and asked who I was? I replied that I was the consultant delivering the training course today, at which point she looked me up and down and said, "Who are you to be a consultant?" I replied that I had worked as a manager for ten years and had a Post Graduate Diploma in Human Resource Management. She then asked me if I wanted a coffee or a tea. I felt I had to justify myself to this person, because I was looking at myself through her eyes. "Yes, who am I to think that I am a consultant?"

A few years passed and I had managed to win work from several organizations. On one occasion I had been contracted to deliver training for an organization which the director wanted us to co-deliver.

He opened the session and introduced us both, giving our names, and then said, "Yes, when Olive and I deliver together everyone calls us the 'Black and White Minstrel Show'." I was mortified, and so were the delegates, who all looked down at the carpet and wouldn't meet my eyes. If this happened now, I would challenge that behaviour but at that time I was just starting out and needed the work, so I just said nothing and carried on.

Another example of an occasion where I felt that I was not valued happened when we won a contract to design and deliver a programme for managers and staff. This was a big contract, training approximately 800 employees nationally, and due to the amount of work we had five associate consultants working with us. Part of the service we offer to clients is that our programmes are bespoke and tailored to their specific needs, and it is important that we demonstrate our knowledge of their business and their concerns to ensure staff feel committed to the training programme. We therefore spend a lot of time getting to know our clients and interviewing staff to get their point of view. We take a diagonal slice of the business, starting with senior managers, line managers, and on through all levels of staff and as a consequence, in this case, we visited six different offices around the country to interview employees as part of our preparation.

I chose Birmingham as the office I would visit, and I knew the Operations Director had contacted each site to ensure that they were expecting us. I arrived fully "suited and booted", as they say. I parked my car and although it was chilly I thought I would soon be inside so didn't put my coat on.

I approached the reception, which had a large glass window at the front, and rang the bell, giving my details via the intercom. I smiled at the woman sitting in reception and announced who I was and who I wanted to see. She abruptly asked me if the manager in question was expecting me, which I confirmed. She did not smile back but left her desk and disappeared for ten minutes, leaving me standing there shivering.

When she returned, she informed me that the manager in question did not recognise my name so I asked her to check her emails from the Operations Director, which confirmed my arrival and why I was visiting the office. Finally, she let me into the office. The whole process had taken twenty minutes and I was freezing. I asked her why, when she could see me through the glass, she didn't let me into the office to keep warm whilst questioning me. She looked me in the eye and said, "I thought you were a Jehovah's Witness", which she obviously felt was ample justification for her rudeness.

I have many examples of similar situations that made me feel devalued and underappreciated, ignored or overlooked. I have had conversations with potential clients on the phone agreeing to visit them to discuss their needs but on arrival being asked, "So where is Olive Strachan?", and then, when I confirmed that I was Olive Strachan, the meeting would be cut short and when I subsequently called back, they were unavailable.

An article in *People Management* magazine, published on 5th February 2019 by Victoria Sprott, describes imposter syndrome as a form of anxiety in which the sufferer finds it hard to accept achievements and success. Her article states that it has been estimated that this affects seven in ten people at some point in their lives. At the time she wrote her article she informed us that, "

In the UK, it is thought that two-thirds of women have suffered from it at work in the last 12 months". Another article, posted in *HR News* on 2nd April 2019, describes imposter syndrome as the, "overwhelming feeling of crippling self-doubt and dread", and they quote a report by *Access Commercial Finance* which stated that a whopping 62% of people at work have been impacted by imposter syndrome and that two thirds of all women will be affected at some stage in their careers. The causes of imposter syndrome are "self-generated self-doubt, being criticised, having to ask for help and comparing ourselves to others".

Trying to build a business meant that I had to put myself out there every day, ringing potential clients, attending meetings and networking, which meant I was being rejected and criticised on a daily basis. I had to work on my self-esteem every day and find a way to build myself up.

Imposter Syndrome Strategy

1. I remind myself of past success, e.g. positive feedback I have received. I keep a record of positive client feedback and read it when I feel low.
2. I recite mantras in my head - "Yes you can!"
3. I visualise a positive outcome, e.g. if I am going to a meeting I visualise myself coming out of the meeting smiling, having won the contract.
4. I dress in clothes that make me feel good; looking good makes me feel good!
5. I put in a lot of preparation, either about the person or the organization. When I am well prepared it increases my confidence.

One of my main challenges is my personality. Those who know me describe me as an extravert, I love to laugh, and most days wake up feeling a sense of joy at being alive! Unfortunately, some people mistake this for flippancy, and presume that I don't take things seriously enough and am therefore lacking in substance.

I am a professional and have learned to adjust to different situations but throughout my life, starting with the nuns at primary school who smacked me with the ruler for being too exuberant, to my poor parents who were not quite sure what to do with this very gregarious child, I have attempted to fit in, to dumb down, to not be myself. It has taken me many years to understand and appreciate who I am, to understand that you don't have to follow the herd and that it's okay not to fit in!

Personality Profiling Tools

One method of helping me to understand my personality, my behaviour and the behaviour of others was using personality profiling tools. These, along with other methods, are used by organizations to ensure that the person they recruit has a personality that will align with and fit into their organization's culture. These tools are also used to assess a person's ability to lead and motivate, and their degree of empathy with others.

There is a wide variety of personality assessment tools and over the years I have found that different organizations have favoured different ones. As a consultant working with senior leadership teams, the first step before working with them on a project is to analyse the makeup of the team and look for any gaps that could cause an imbalance, thus impacting on the team's successful completion of a task or project. This involves completing a questionnaire which is then analysed.

The results are shared with the individual and sometimes, with their consent, shared between the whole team, which helps to deepen the understanding of one another's strengths and possible areas of conflict.

There are many profiling tools but the tool that resonates the most with me and with my international delegates is TetraMap, because it is memorable. It also helps to create a common language that focuses on the positive attributes of individuals and helps others to understand and value the differences in people. It gives some clarity about why an individual behaves the way they do.

TetraMap is a tool that was created by Yoshimi & John Brett. They spent most of their time in New Zealand which is where they were inspired by the landscape to study the concept of the four elements as a profiling tool. The TetraMap®tool measures our preferences, not necessarily our strengths. It is a learning model used by organizations including BBC Worldwide, NASA, O2, Lidl, Deutsche Bank and Sainsbury's Argos, which looks to nature to increase personal well-being and team cohesion.

I have used this tool with executives, for team leader training and coaching. At the heart of TetraMap is the belief that strength lies in valuing differences. The elements TetraMap uses are rooted in nature: Earth, Air, Water and Fire. Every element has a part to play. When you complete the short questionnaire, you find out what your highest preferences are. Each one of us is a unique mix of the four elements, and our low scoring preferences are just as significant as the high scoring preferences. The Element Descriptors are as follows:

Earth: Bold and sturdy, confident in the way they walk and talk. Goals, control, achievement and winning are important. Quick, possibly risky decisions come easily.
Air: These orderly and focused individuals rely on their abilities to think things out. They excel in finding logical solutions and making sense of situations. They listen and plan to ensure accuracy and quality.
Water: Caring and consistent, they are vital in holding families and teams together. They are loyal and deeply feeling people who show steadfast effort, great patience and a desire for harmony and flow.
Fire: Looking at the positive side of life, they love to explore possibilities and inspire others to see bright futures. They are colourful, love variety and have a great sense of fun!

I have been an accredited TetraMap facilitator for over ten years. The results of my completed questionnaire demonstrate that I am high Fire and then Earth, with Water next and Air being my lowest score. I have used this analysis to help me understand myself and how I interact with others, and how this impacts on my leadership skills. I have often recruited my own staff to fill the gaps of my weaker elements.

CHAPTER 7

BUSINESS CHALLENGES

The business was growing and I needed to recruit staff, so having years of recruitment experience I thought this would be easy. When I worked in the industry I was recruiting on behalf of large, reputable organizations offering good salaries and enticing remuneration packages. I was a small business offering someone the opportunity to grow with me. This proved tempting in the short term, mainly to students wanting their first job, but as soon as they had something to write on their C.V.'s they would move on.

I made many mistakes and the worst one was recruiting someone that I had met on a training course. I needed someone to help deal with clients who needed training resources and to deal with enquiries, whilst I dealt with sales and client meetings; she seemed like a lovely girl. However, the nature of my job meant I was hardly in the office, I was either meeting clients or delivering training or coaching, so when I returned to the office unexpectedly one day I was surprised to find a strange man in my office, with my office administrator typing and photocopying for him. He had developed a habit of coming into my office and asking for pieces of work to be done and I had to ask him not to enter my office in future, unless I specifically invited him to do so. I then realised that my office assistant had been neglecting my work whilst helping this other organization and she had no commitment to me or my business. I had also received client complaints about calling the office and the phone not being answered, and invoices and paperwork not being sent out promptly, so I took the decision to terminate her employment and ask her to leave, which she didn't take very well.

During our time together I had frequently given her lifts in my car, either to joint meetings or just taking her home. That evening I went to collect my car from its normal parking place only to find it had been damaged.

There were big gouges in the paintwork which looked like a coin had been used, my tyres had been deflated, headlights kicked and broken, etc. She had boasted frequently about knowing some very unsavoury characters. I couldn't drive it home and had to get the insurance company to collect it. Thankfully, I never heard from her or saw her again.

Finding the right staff can be challenging for a fledgling business and over the years I have recruited friends and family to help me. Eventually, using personality profiling to understand myself better and the type of staff I needed to fill the gaps, I built a strong team to support me, and by understanding and clarifying my business values and mission I recruited people aligned to the OSR brand.

My confidence in my business was growing. The resource centre was busy with clients frequently booking in to view resources, I was designing and delivering training courses for clients and being asked to speak at client events, and I finally had a member of staff that I could trust. I felt I had a viable business and the next step was growth.

I had been out to visit a new client and upon returning to my serviced office on Deansgate I found two strange men in reception. They informed me that they were bailiffs and that the entire building would be closed and padlocked by Monday morning - this was Thursday afternoon! When I asked why this was happening, as I had paid my rent and the prerequisite deposit, I was informed that the landlord had not paid the rent for the building and they were therefore taking possession of it and closing it down. As a courtesy they were giving us some warning.

I had two offices at the time, one office containing all my training resources including books, games, learning packs and resources, all in all about 500 items, none of which actually belonged to me as I was acting as an agent for different suppliers.

Contractually I was responsible for all these resources. The other office contained all my client files, cabinets, etc. I went into a complete panic.

How was I going to move all these resources over a weekend, ready for Monday when I had a client coming to view and with a large budget to spend? More importantly, where was I going to move them to? I had just paid my rent for that month and I was owed my deposit, which I was told I would not be getting back.

I spent a lot of time on the phone calling various serviced office companies and thankfully I managed to secure space at a large complex called 'The Triangle' in Manchester, although I had to pay a deposit plus a month's rent in advance before I could move in. I was given the key to my offices and access to the external doors that allowed entry to my specific area of the building. The Manchester business community is very close knit and I was not the only organization looking to move quickly; I recognised a few of the organizations based in my old offices that had also made the move to the Triangle. (The Triangle eventually reverted to its original name of "The Corn Exchange" and following a change of use it is now famous for its bars and restaurants.)

I now had new offices, but how was I going to transport all the physical stock and resources that I had in just three days? I couldn't afford to hire a removal service, so my husband and I hired a van and together with a friend of his, Tosh Assueni, we managed to move everything ourselves. Sometimes in a crisis your friends are not always available, and you have to just get on with it.

We came into the office at 6am, stopped for necessary food and comfort breaks, and then continued working until the early hours of the morning. Our goal was to empty the old office, then move all the resources and set up the resource library and the office ready for the client on the Monday morning - and we did it! I can't describe my stress levels over that weekend, and how grateful I was to my husband and his friend, because there is no way I could have done that on my own.

CHAPTER 8

THE RECESSION OF 2008

It is now 2008. I have two serviced offices in the Triangle, I employ four staff and the business has two income streams: OSR, the resource centre offering clients viewing facilities for videos, books, business games and simulations; and Olive Strachan Consultancy, which encompasses the design and delivery of training courses, including coaching and mentoring services. I have approximately seven freelance consultants that I use for large contracts. I have a bookkeeper working for me and I employ an accountant, as OSR is a Limited Company. I use a company that provides I.T. support and another that supports my website. Once again things are going to plan, and I am looking at possibly purchasing rather than renting offices and growing my business to the next level. Then the phone stopped ringing, and there were no enquiries coming through – the country was heading for a recession.

The recession in Britain and across the world was a direct result of the credit crunch that began in August 2007 and which worsened dramatically into a global financial crisis in the autumn of 2008. I must admit I was ill-prepared for the recession. I kept telling myself that it was a glitch and things would soon get back to normal. I had worked with other organizations to assist them in leading their staff through challenging times, so I put all my knowledge to good use. I had regular meetings with my team to explain the situation we were facing, we made sure that each staff member was playing to their strengths; we put a plan in place to ensure that we communicated with clients on a regular basis and we had sales campaigns and promotions.

All this was to no avail because most businesses in the UK were facing exactly the same situation and had gone into survival mode. The last thing they wanted, or were financially able to do, was to invest in staff training; they were focusing on paying wages and keeping people in work.

As the months went by, I had to make my own staff redundant and this included members of my family who were working for me at the time, which was difficult and soul destroying. I had to speak to all my creditors and ask them to support me through these tough times. Some reduced payments, my accountant allowed me some breathing space, but my bookkeeper had to go. Gradually, I went through all my savings and then went into debt. I wasn't sleeping and I used to wake up in the middle of the night with my heart racing and finding it hard to breathe with anxiety, and then my hair started to fall out, resulting in a bald patch. I became extremely boring to be around, my only conversation was about the business, the problems I was having, and not being able to deal with it. Most people advised me to walk away from the business; it wasn't working so why was I bothering?

Despite all that was happening around me, I knew I was not the only person experiencing this and it never occurred to me to give up. I had reached rock bottom, with my husband investing some money in the business to keep it afloat, but that soon went because there were just not enough sales being made to make the business viable. They do say that when a recession hits the first thing that organizations cut back on is staff training, which I learned to my cost.

In the midst of this, I sat down and analysed the situation. Yes, it was a global recession, but there were parts of the world that had not been impacted by this and the Middle East, for example, was still doing extremely well. I had worked internationally before, so I went through my client database, seeking out clients that were based internationally who might be able to use my skills.

I had previously worked for the British Council and they had a hundred offices around the world so I focused all my efforts into attracting the interest of these international clients, sending out mail shots, brochures, course details and calling wherever possible. Suddenly I received an email enquiry asking me to put forward a proposal to design and deliver a programme of four modules for fifty managers in the Middle East, to be delivered over an eight-month period.

I sat at my desk, heart thumping and determined to win this contract. I had to devise a plan that would ensure that this client would choose me! I contacted the Department for International Trade (DIT) for advice on cultural norms and how best to close deals with different cultures; I knew that building trust was extremely important. When discussing requirements with the client, I asked what was important to her regarding the organization she would allocate the contract to, and she told me that understanding the organization was key! I felt well-placed, as I had worked with the British Council for nearly ten years, firstly providing training resources and then delivering training. The second thing the client wanted was an organization with the necessary expertise that she could trust to deliver a quality programme. At the time, I didn't find it as easy to build trust over an email or Skype and I realised that a face to face meeting was the only way forward. I used my credit card and purchased a flight to Egypt, even though it was to be a short visit – a meeting with the client, one night in a hotel and fly back again the next day. Fortunately, the meeting went well and although the client did not confirm straight away, as I sat on the plane returning to the UK I knew that I had done everything in my power to win the contract.

A few weeks later I was thrilled to receive confirmation that my proposal had been successful. It was the most satisfying experience, as I knew that this contract was going to save my business.

The client who confirmed that we had won the contract was Irene Riad, who continued to use my services on other projects. I have kept in contact with Irene and we are in discussion at the moment about some potential work.

I realised at the time that if this project was successful it would not only be the Middle East that would use OSR. The British Council has offices around the world, I was training managers, future directors, this was a superb opportunity and I worked with one of our freelance designers to ensure that this bespoke programme would meet the client's needs.

CHAPTER 9

GOING GLOBAL

My international career started in the year 2000. My recruitment experience meant that a lot of my early training work was designing and delivering courses in sales, recruitment and selection, influencing skills and negotiation. I had designed and delivered a successful sales training programme for a company called Terminix and the client feedback was that they had seen an increase in sales after my training course. I was then asked to travel to Ireland, and then Amsterdam.

I have worked internationally for many companies including Terminix, Campanile Hotels and Brand Addition, but the bulk of my international work has been with the British Council. As I said earlier the relationship developed from selling resources to delivering training. It began with assertiveness skills training and eventually performance management. I started with the Manchester office but as my network of contacts increased I received an enquiry from the London office and began delivering training at their Spring Gardens location. I seemed to have a connection with the British Council and their staff, I started to receive enquiries from the British Council in Wales and Ireland, and then globally. When I asked how they had heard about OSR, they said that I had been recommended to them by other offices. As I was trying to grow and establish my business, this was music to my ears!

Then something happened which would have a long-term effect on me and my business. The British Council had designed a training programme called "The Management Foundation Programme", which was a five-day workshop for new managers covering "Your World". This focused on you as a manager, your values etc., then managing relationships, managing change, managing time, managing stress, action planning and goal setting.

The team from the British Council who had designed this workshop spent some time with me, taking me through the programme so that I was clear on what they wanted to achieve and the outcomes for the delegates. I believe it was one of the best courses I have ever delivered; I wanted to make sure that I did justice to the team who had designed it, but ultimately to the delegates attending the course.

This began around 2004 and was when I discovered that although I loved delivering training, management development training was the specific area that I was really drawn to and would like to focus on. I remember being a line manager myself and the challenges I had to face. Being a line manager sometimes feels like you are between a rock and a hard place. Your team see you as 'management' therefore you are no longer part of them, and you are not part of the senior management team either.

It can feel very lonely, particularly if you are promoted amongst your peers. This happened to me when I worked in recruitment in the 1980s, I used to go home and cry on my husband's shoulder until I learned some valuable lessons.

Lesson number one: as a manager you will not always be liked; lesson number two: just having the title of manager does not mean that you instantly earn respect.

Lesson number three: sometimes you have to have those difficult conversations that are unpleasant, but it's your job to do it; Lesson number four: keep things in perspective - in a hundred years' time all the petty things you are worrying about won't matter! So, I toughened up!

The first time I delivered this programme there were twenty-five managers who had been flown into the UK from all over the world. As the British Council has a hundred offices around the world, I had a mixture of culture, ages and genders and whilst delivering this programme I learned many things.

Firstly, I would have benefited from a similar course many years ago, it would definitely have helped me to be a better manager.

Secondly, I learned about culture; all these managers had the same job description and standards of work but because of the country they lived in, and the different cultures, this would impact on how they managed their staff. These delegates arrived as strangers but when they left after five days, they had built alliances and strong relationships with one other, and with me. I continued to deliver this programme for a number of years, and some of the managers I trained are now Country Directors within the British Council.

During the 2008 recession I was still working for the British Council on an ad hoc basis but it was not enough to sustain my business. Winning the international contract to train over 50 managers over an eight-month period was a lifeline. Without this contract I would not be in business today. During this period, I was contacted by many training companies looking for collaborations or trying to sell their companies to me; we were all drowning, and many consultancies I was in contact with then no longer exist.

I was also thinking of the long-term benefits of growing my international market and increasing sales, so that when the recession was over I wouldn't be solely reliant on the UK market. I spent some time reflecting on where I was now in the global market, where I would like to be and how I was going to get there. My first action was to ensure that winning this contract didn't go unnoticed, so I contacted the Manchester Evening News again, reminded them that when I first opened my business they were kind enough to write about me and that, ten years on, I had just won my first major global contract. Once again, they supported me by publishing a story about my success.

I recognised that there was a gap in my knowledge of exporting, and of cultural awareness, and I knew it was important to gain the skills and knowledge necessary to be a success if I was to grow my business internationally. I joined the Department for International Trade (DIT) and was allocated an international trade adviser. The DIT has experts who can help with culture, language, marketing, etc.

They also organise trade fares in your particular market and have a service where one-to-one meetings can be arranged with potential clients. Receiving this support really boosted my confidence and having the support of the DIT was invaluable whilst growing my international business; they are a great source of helpful contacts and have many opportunities for businesses to network together. I attended a trade fare organised by the DIT in Barbados and Trinidad and Tobago, which allowed me to make contacts with education and training providers in these countries, and I was subsequently offered a contract in Trinidad as a result of this.

Working internationally has had a big impact on me, both personally and professionally. It is said that travelling, particularly to a foreign country, can help you re-evaluate and reinvent your life and I have found this to be true.

I realised that I had a lot of preconceived ideas regarding different cultures and working internationally was a big learning curve for me. Something I found helpful was knowing that some organizations look after their consultants by sending out information regarding cultural norms and essential advice before you travel. I would recommend this as an important part of the preparation. Even then, you can still get it wrong!

I have travelled extensively around the Middle East, Turkey, Cyprus, Egypt, and the territories of Arabia proper, including Kuwait, Yemen, Oman, Bahrain and Dubai. I have visited Muscat in Oman on numerous occasions and before travelling I was sure to read up about the dress code and cultural norms. Previously I have delivered training for the British Council and British Embassy, but on this assignment, in 2016, I was working for a different organization.

Whilst working in the Middle East I opt for a formal business suit, which is very modest with a high neckline, a jacket to cover my arms, a long skirt, and I have a scarf readily available. The training is normally in a hotel where there are many international visitors, some of whom do not always adhere to the dress code of the country.

I arrived on the first day of training and looking around in the canteen where I was having a cup of coffee, and I felt that my attire was appropriate. However, on entering the training room, the atmosphere was quite frosty, and it wasn't because of the air conditioning! After day one of the course, as I was preparing to go to my hotel, the person who organised the training offered to drive me and on the way told me she was not happy with the length of my skirt, it needed to be longer. In other words, touching the floor. Also, she had not taken to my boisterous personality and wanted me to subdue it a little.

That evening, whilst preparing for day two of the training course, I examined my wardrobe looking for something suitable.

Fortunately, I had packed a long summer dress which touched the floor and therefore fitted the bill, but it also revealed my cleavage so I had to fasten my jacket over it, right to the top. I felt like a trussed-up turkey in that heat! I could accommodate the client regarding my attire, however, it's not easy to change my personality.

I did try to be quiet and more subdued the following day, but in the end you cannot change your personality. The main thing is to respect not only a country's norms, but also those of the individual organization that you are working for. This is not necessary everywhere, but this particular client did require this, and I was happy to comply.

The key here is to listen to the feedback, apologise if you get it wrong and make the appropriate changes. My advice would be that each country is individual, do your research as to what is acceptable. Etiquette in more cosmopolitan Dubai, for example, may not be the same in other countries. Also, try to gauge the organization's dress code. Having visited the Middle East on numerous occasions I was confident that I was dressed appropriately, but this particular client had exacting standards and it was something that I needed to know. It is important to learn from your mistakes – and if you get it wrong, apologise and fix it!

Travel definitely broadens the mind and gives you a different perspective as you are confronted with new experiences, and I have travelled extensively for work and pleasure. My work has allowed me to visit countries that I never thought I would see in my lifetime and has given me the confidence to push myself further than I previously thought possible. I would encourage anyone who wants to build their confidence to travel because facing difficulties in an unfamiliar environment and amongst strangers forces you to learn and adapt to circumstances outside your comfort zone.

This can increase your focus, creativity and drive, and long term can help you become more flexible, patient and emotionally strong.

I wanted to share this with you because I am certain that working globally and travelling internationally at every opportunity has unequivocally contributed to my success.

I must admit that every time I was asked to work internationally it gave me a frisson of excitement. I felt lucky and privileged to see the world and get paid for it! My clients would book me into lovely hotels and although I was alone, I loved sitting by the pool or the ocean, or on my balcony, soaking up the beautiful vistas. Not all my travel experiences were like this, some clients' budgets meant that the accommodation was not luxurious, but it was always comfortable.

The most difficult thing for me when working abroad was what to do with myself when I wasn't working. Some contracts meant that I might only be working for two or three days a week, over several weeks. I had no friends in these countries and was reliant on the client or the delegates I was working with to also be my companions.

Over the years I have been fortunate to make the acquaintance of very kind and generous people who put themselves out to make sure I was okay, many of whom I am still in contact with.

My lovely friend, Dalia Adel from the British Council, has given me her time in abundance, from our first meeting in Kuwait when she organised to take me sightseeing and out for dinner, to horse riding in the desert, a trip to Alexandria and a felucca ride down the River Nile in Egypt - a felucca is a traditional wooden sailing boat. Oh, the beauty of gently sailing down the Nile at sunset! It was an amazing experience that is embedded in my memory forever.

On another occasion, one of the managers from the British Council, Azza Farag, took the weekend away from her family to give me a sightseeing tour around Bahrain. Larisa Halilovic, a Director for the British Council, has given me the opportunity to work with her on more than one occasion in Bosnia and Herzegovina, and whenever I visit I receive a warm welcome and the opportunity to sample the local food and spend time in her company. I must also mention Andrew Glass, Director British Council Thailand, who used my services when he was based in Montenegro, and more recently in Bangkok. Andrew is an exceptional host, taking me on sightseeing tours and out for delicious meals. Finally, I must mention Caroline Morrisey, based in Switzerland. Whilst working with Caroline she invited me to her home, where her husband cooked us a beautiful meal. Travelling abroad alone has taught me how kind and generous people can be. My heart has always been warmed by the kindness of strangers, people who don't know me but put my welfare and comfort first. I value kindness above all things.

This isn't to say that I haven't also experienced quite challenging situations during my trips abroad, albeit ones that have made me more aware, as well as stronger and more resilient.

I was able to visit Yemen twice during 2008, to deliver leadership and management training, before the situation in that country became as desperate as it is today. I found it to be very different from the rest of the Middle East, after the luxury and opulence of Dubai, Bahrain, etc., in fact it was quite a shock. As I was driven through the capital, Sanaa, I noticed that a lot of the men seemed to have one cheek protruding slightly and I asked the driver why this was. He told me they were chewing 'gat'.

The Khat plant, known as gat in Yemen, has been grown for use as a stimulant for centuries in the horn of Africa and Arabian Peninsula.

Chewing gat predates the use of coffee and is used in a similar social context, so when walking around Yemen it was quite normal to see people chewing 'gat'.

My hotel was comfortable but outside there were armed guards, part of the security measures to prevent the kidnapping of foreigners which was common at that time. There were also challenges with delivering the training because the electricity would regularly cut out without warning and we would be left in complete darkness. Visual projected slides etc. would disappear so I had to just keep on talking and eventually the electricity would return and we would carry on as normal.

My downtime in Yemen was very restrictive; there were no English channels on the television, so I spent most of my time sitting in reception, reading or people watching. In complete contrast, when I visited Qatar and Dubai I could go out for a walk if I was bored or restless, visit a museum, have a coffee, or go the mall and do some shopping.

One evening, after having been taken to dinner by my host, we were walking back to the hotel and happened to pass a Yemeni wedding. I was fascinated to see that the men were all together with the groom, and the bride was separate with all the women, so very different from the weddings I was used to in the UK. My hosts were kind enough to organise a sightseeing tour for me and I asked if we could drive out so that I could see some of the landscape, which we did, but after a while we were stopped by armed men and the driver had to show a document to prove that we were allowed to drive in that particular area.

Sanaa is an ancient city and there was beauty in its fascinating history. Standing in this ancient, dry, crumbling city is something that I will never forget. The lack of freedom was challenging but it is somewhere that I am pleased that I had the opportunity to visit.

In 2006 I was invited by the British Council in Portugal to deliver a management development programme to twenty delegates. I invited one of my freelance training associates to accompany me, as it was a large group over three days, and we were both looking forward to our trip. We had sent out pre-course questionnaires, which the delegates had returned to us, so we already began to feel a connection with them. We planned in meticulous detail our training programme, the exercises and the handouts that we were going to supply to the delegates. I believe it is very important to present yourself well and live up to your brand and I had had some beautiful folders printed for the delegates, complete with my company logo.

My associate and I had frequent meetings prior to the trip, planning how the three days' training would flow and who would deliver which part of the programme. We arrived at the airport; I was dressed in my suit, as I would be meeting the client within a few hours, and my associate dressed in a smart casual manner. The training packs were heavy, so we packed them in our suitcases which had to be checked in, and we had minimal hand luggage.

After a very pleasant flight we arrived in Portugal, proceeded through customs and waited expectantly at the luggage carousel...and waited...and waited. After all the other passengers had picked up their luggage, we realised that our luggage was not there. We reported it to the appropriate people and were told to come back tomorrow, meanwhile they would make enquires on our behalf. The only problem was that we would not be there tomorrow, the training programme was being held in a different location and we would be away for about three days, and what's more we had no course materials with us!

As I sat in the taxi on the way to meet our client, I felt very agitated. I needed to print off twenty delegate packs ready for a training course the following day and because our props, toys and materials for the course were also in our suitcases, I would have to find a way to rework our exercises without the materials we had already purchased.

My main concern was that my client, who was paying handsomely for my services, did not feel that the quality of service was compromised. Thankfully the client was sympathetic and we were able to print the necessary delegate packs from the one copy I had in my hand luggage. We were then driven to our location a few hours' drive away from Lisbon. I met with my associate and we planned how we were going to deliver the training without our missing materials and how we could make sure that the client experience was a positive one. It also dawned on us that we didn't have a change of clothes, all we had was what we were standing up in. Luckily I don't wear a lot of makeup and had my lipstick in my handbag, but unfortunately for my colleague all her makeup was in her suitcase and she was concerned about not looking her best for the delegates the next day. When we arrived at the hotel, we had the evening free, so we hired a taxi and went to a clothes shop but - unfortunately for us - the typical Portuguese woman is quite petite, and we were two 'voluptuous' women and couldn't find anything to fit us!

We spent the next few days delivering a training programme that delegates found engaging, motivational and fun, whilst our evenings were spent washing our clothes and drying them for the following day, reworking our course to fill the missing materials and adjusting the programme accordingly.

On our last day we asked for feedback from the delegates, which was extremely positive. Only then did we share with them the situation regarding our lost suitcases, how we'd had to think on our feet regarding the missing materials and had to wash our clothes out every evening, ready for the following day. They were amazed and commented that our level of customer service was so high that they'd had no inkling of the challenges we had overcome.

It was a painful lesson to learn but you can imagine that when I travel now I always have my training materials with me in a little carry-on case, and a few days' essential changes of clothes.

In April 2010 I had bookings to deliver our leadership and management programme in Tashkent, Uzbekistan, and I had completed my visa applications, giving the details of when I would be arriving and leaving the country. However, the volcanic events at Eyjafjallajökull in Iceland, although relatively small, caused enormous disruption to air travel across western and northern Europe over an initial period of six days in April 2010. This had an unforeseen impact on my trip and has left a lasting memory.

When I arrived at Manchester airport to begin my journey the airport was crowded, and you couldn't see the floor because there were so many people waiting for news of their flights. Finally, we were informed that due to the ash cloud we would not be flying that evening as scheduled, but coaches would take us to Birmingham. The travel operator would arrange flights from Birmingham for the following day and overnight accommodation would be provided. I remember the BBC crew filming the situation as our coach left the airport. We did fly out the following day, so I thought no more about it, I was just anxious to get to my destination.

I arrived in Uzbekistan and the course went well. Everyone was welcoming, warm and very hospitable. Each morning, when the delegates arrived, someone would bring freshly baked bread from their particular region and it would be shared out and enjoyed by all. I thought this was a lovely tradition and a special way to start the day. During my stay I visited the beautiful city of Samarkand which is known for its mosques and mausoleums. It is on the Silk Road, the ancient trade route linking China to the Mediterranean, and it was an extremely memorable experience.

At the conclusion of the programme I was escorted to the airport and taken straight to check in. I waved goodbye to the young man who had brought me to the airport and proceeded to go through check in and on to immigration. When I arrived at passport control the official behind the counter looked at me, then looked at my passport and called someone over. He pointed at me and told me to leave the counter and go and stand in a corner.

I had passed all my paperwork to this person, including all my contact details for my client and local telephone numbers. I kept asking what was wrong but no one would speak to me. I stood there for about thirty minutes, although it felt like thirty hours, watching as other people went through passport control and on towards the aircraft. Time was running out because there were only two flights per week and if I missed this one I would have to wait another two days, with nowhere to stay in the meantime. I approached the desk again and tentatively asked what the problem was, only to be informed that there was an issue with my visa.

I heard the final boarding call for my flight and my anxiety levels escalated. As I was standing there, looking anxious and worried, a man passed me on his way through passport control and he paused to ask me, "What's wrong, honey?"

I told him I'd been asked to stand there as my visa was out of date and he cheerfully said, "Oh they throw you in prison here for lesser offences than that!", and with that he smiled and went off to board the plane. I immediately went from slightly anxious to mild panic! All I had in my hand was my mobile phone, so I rang my daughter Rhia, in the UK, who was working as my Office/HR Manager in the business at that time, and tearfully told her about my situation. Within no time my client had been contacted, along with the British Embassy, and after a one-to-one meeting in a room with a customs official, where I was reprimanded for not checking and extending my visa appropriately, I was allowed to continue on my way.

I can't tell you how relieved I was to finally board that plane! I subsequently realised that the flight delay due to the volcanic ash cloud had impacted on my arrival and leaving dates, and I had stayed in the country beyond the date on my visa. From that day forward I always double check the dates on my visas and make sure that they match my arrival and departure dates.

I have visited Muscat in Oman for many years, my first visit was in 2005 and I visited another eight times up to 2016.

I love Muscat, it is very beautiful and over the years I have made some good friends who are based there. I stay in a lovely hotel with gorgeous views, and when I am not working I thoroughly enjoy the ambiance. I usually visit the Grand Mosque, or go to the souk; I have also visited the Sultan's palace. It is somewhere I always look forward to visiting. On one of my visits a few years back, I was based there for about a week or so. In between delivering training I was a little restless, so I approached the reception of the hotel and asked if they could recommend anything I could do after work to amuse myself.

I was given a brochure for a sunset cruise, which sounded fabulous! I could see myself on deck, mingling with other people and sipping a drink whilst we gazed at the beautiful sunset, so I went ahead and booked.

At the appointed time I prepared myself by covering my head and making sure that I was dressed appropriately, according to local customs. A young man arrived in a car and picked me up and took me to my location. I stood at the jetty, looking with appreciation at the sea. He asked me to wait there and told me the boat would be along shortly. To my surprise the same young man then pulled up to the jetty in a canoe. I climbed in gingerly, thinking that we would use this canoe to take me to the larger boat with the rest of the party. Then he welcomed me to my sunset tour, and I realised that this was it! As we moved off into a rather dark and choppy sea, I was thrown around the canoe like a rag doll. I looked around for life jackets, as I can't swim, and when I couldn't see anything vaguely resembling a life jacket, I began to feel slightly alarmed. I said a silent prayer, wondering if I'd ever get off the canoe safely.

With some trepidation I told my companion that it was not quite what I expected and that I didn't want to go on the tour, but he reassured me that it was quite safe and told me that if I cancelled the tour he would be severely out of pocket and his family were relying on him, so I agreed to go ahead.

By now it was late afternoon and the sea was getting more and more choppy; the boat started to rock and I was thrown from side to side, at one point nearly rolling over completely.

I was drenched from head to toe, cold, wet and disgruntled and I kept saying, "It's okay, we can cut the tour short and return to shore!", but he insisted that as I had paid for one hour he wanted to make sure I got value for money! The waves were so choppy that I felt quite shaken, and when I asked about my promised soft drink, he opened a cooler box and gave me a can of coke!

Finally, it was over, and I was helped back into the car, shivering from head to toe and drenched in sea water. I went back to the hotel and normally I would have been reluctant to sit in the main restaurant on my own, but after that experience I sat down at a table for one, looking very bedraggled and not caring one bit. I ordered a lovely meal and the largest glass of red wine - after that experience I felt in need of some comfort.

Since then, whenever I travel and book any excursions, I always speak to the official travel representative first and ask for their specific recommendations, check for details and reviews on the internet, and so minimise the risk of another "sunset cruise"!

On a rare occasion I have been genuinely frightened whist travelling. I was in Karachi, just after some bombings had taken place, and was collected from the airport in an armoured vehicle. I received a briefing about what to do in the event of another bomb going off and the car was then checked, complete with sniffer dogs, before we climbed in. It really was quite scary, but it did not detract from the warm hospitality I received during my visit. Once security was taken care of, I thoroughly enjoyed my visit and came away having learned more about the culture of Pakistan.

When you are travelling abroad you can't always predict what is going to happen. My advice is to read all the information you can before making your journey, listen to the advice you are given and follow instructions. Hire a local tour guide if you can, it's a shame to visit a country and not experience local culture and taste the national dishes.

There are some key lessons I have learned during my travels as an international training consultant: explore and immerse yourself in the culture of the country you are visiting; acquaint yourself with the laws and social etiquette – you have to adjust to the country, not the other way around; try to learn a few basics phrases of the language.

For example, I usually learn how to say good morning, hello, or a few sentences; and be aware of cultural sensitivities, in particular regarding dress codes.

I mentioned earlier that I had joined the DIT. I signed up for the *Passport to Export* programme which is an export assessment and support programme for small and medium-sized enterprises (SME). It provides new or inexperienced exporters with training, planning and support to grow their business overseas. They also have the *Overseas Market Introduction Service* (OMIS), which can help your business at any stage of exporting, from finding opportunities to setting up in another country. OMIS can put your organization in touch directly with DIT staff in over 100 overseas markets. It can help you to access the right international contacts or partners, find the best way to do business in a specific market, achieve a successful market entry strategy, and increase profits by using effective overseas promotion. I have taken advantage of both these services and would highly recommend that anyone wanting to build an international business gets in touch with the DIT.

CHAPTER 10

STEPS TO SUCCESS

Manchester 2002 – Commonwealth Games

Working with the Commonwealth Games Committee when they were in Manchester was one of the highlights of my career. They came to view the training video called "Fish!" which I have mentioned earlier in this book. They wanted to use it as part of the training for volunteers to demonstrate what superb customer service looked like.

Whilst viewing the video we started talking and I asked which trainers they were going to use to deliver the training, and if I could be considered. I was informed that various companies were pitching for the business, I needed to submit a proposal and if they were interested I would be called in to deliver a presentation.

My course designer and I prepared a 45-minute, interactive session; our pitch was successful, and I ended up training hundreds of volunteers for the Commonwealth Games. It was an exciting and exhilarating experience, working with volunteers from around the world, all coming together with an equal passion for making the games the best ever, and I was thrilled when a film crew arrived to record one of my training sessions for a piece to be transmitted on the local television evening news. I have lived in Manchester now for thirty years and I was so proud to be a part of this.

Global Oil and Gas Organisation

When we won a contract from this company, to design and deliver customer services training for approximately 800 employees, we were told they had come to OSR for our particular brand of training.

Prior to delivering the contract we interviewed a cross section of the organization to understand the client's working methodology and we had to co-ordinate five consultants working all over the UK. The real challenge for me was that the client had chosen my consultancy because they liked the way I delivered training - professional, with great content, but also fun and engaging - and it was difficult to find associate consultants with the right fit.

This project lasted for approximately six months and during that time, after receiving continuous client feedback throughout the project, we had to let some associates go and recruit new ones. The lesson from this experience is that clients buy you and your brand, and although an associate consultant recruited for a specific contract may be qualified and have the knowledge and excellent references, it is essential that they are also able to convey your brand in order not to disappoint the client.

This feedback was vital in helping to shape how we worked going forward.

The British Council

I have mentioned earlier in my book the importance of aligning yourself with organisations that you feel a connection with or have an admiration for their contribution to the world. The British council is the United Kingdom's international organisation for cultural relations and international opportunities. It builds connections, understanding and trust between people in the UK and other countries through arts and culture, education and the English language.

Winning our global leadership contract with the British Council also involved some work with the British Embassy. This was a definite step to success in helping to build our global brand, gain confidence and develop international contracts, starting in the Middle East and then expanding to include other countries.

Winning an Award for
Achievement in International Business

In 2009 I was honoured for my success in growing my Manchester based company overseas and took home the award for "Achievement in International Business" at a glamorous award show at Manchester United Football Club. My daughter, Rhia Boyode, was working with me as our Office/HR manager at the time and it was lovely to have her collect the award with me.

The prestigious ceremony was organised by the Ethnic Minority Business Forum, part of the North West Regional Development Agency (NWRDA). Hosted by BBC presenter Ranvir Singh, over 400 guests attended the awards including Baroness Valerie Amos, Leader of the House of Lords and first Black woman to be appointed to the British Cabinet, and Steven Broomhead, Chief Executive of the NWRDA. At the event, the winner of each of the six categories was chosen by the audience using voting pads. It was wonderful to receive this award for our efforts!

Chair of the Chartered Institute of Personnel and Development (CIPD)

I became a member of the CIPD when I started my post graduate studies in 1996 and I am still a member today. When I opened my business in 1998, I felt extremely lonely and also, as a new business owner, I needed some help and support. Joining my local CIPD committee in Manchester seemed a wise choice. There were many consultants on the committee and also, as this was the body that would ultimately award my diploma, I wanted to take the opportunity to learn and develop. I offered my services as a volunteer and over time carried out every role on the committee.

At one point I was the group leader for the Altrincham group, which involved arranging a venue for meetings and organising speakers to speak at events.

In my PR/Marketing role I was responsible for promoting and marketing the branch newsletter, and gaining sponsorship opportunities. As Vice Chair my role was to support the Chair and stand in for him whenever he was unavailable. Eventually I became the first Black female Chair in the CIPD. It was a huge challenge, as the Manchester branch is the largest branch outside of London with over 5000 members and 22 committee members.

I was keen to ensure that we lived up to the CIPD's "PACE" values, which are: Purposeful, Agile, Collaborative, and Expert.

The Manchester CIPD branch has a good mix of people with various specialisms and backgrounds and I was proud to be part of it. As the Branch Chair I really wanted to build collaborative relationships with local organizations and ensure that we provided an excellent service to our members.

I learned some valuable lessons in that role, for example all committee members were volunteers, not employees, and it is not always easy to lead volunteers. We had some strong characters that had been on the committee for a lot longer than I had. We had a range of people, from those in their twenties right up to the extremely experienced members in their seventies, who had worked in the HR field for many years. There were changes afoot and these were not always well received. I had a lot to learn, both from the role and from other members. I started out as Branch Chair by having individual one-to-one sessions with everyone to try to understand what they wanted from their role and how I could accommodate their needs. David Redfern, the previous Chair, was an excellent mentor, providing advice and support. All committee members wanted to provide the best service possible for our members and this mutual goal made us a formidable team.

I also received a lot of support from Peter Cheese, who was the new CEO of the CIPD. He was supportive to all Branch Chairs, making himself available for events all over the country.

I have a lot of respect and admiration for Peter, he made a lot of positive changes to the CIPD and every time I see him, I ask him if he will coach me! I think if he said yes to everyone who asked him he wouldn't have time to fulfil his role as CEO, however, Peter has always been supportive of me; he is always encouraging and has taken an interest in my career.

Whilst being Branch Chair I wanted to raise the profile of HR, not least because of a meeting I'd had with the CEO of an organization in Wythenshawe, Manchester. I had been invited by the Director of this company to discuss delivering a training course for them on networking. After we had agreed dates etc., I brought up the CIPD and said that as Branch Chair I would like to invite him to attend one of our events.

His exact words were, "Olive, I would rather stick pins in my eyes than spend my time with HR people!" I had heard this response before.

The impression that many board members and senior directors had of HR was not always a true picture, but a common one. I subsequently spent a lot of time with CIPD committee members building collaborative relationships with businesses. If we move forward to 2020, I believe the role of the HR professional is valued, with many executive boards including an HR professional where they can make a real contribution to the organizational strategic plan, rather than being seen as a problem solver.

I gave a lot of my time and effort as a volunteer and encouraged my clients to get involved in the CIPD. I gained a great deal from this role, it contributed hugely to my personal growth and development, the highlights being Branch Chair during the CIPD centenary celebrations; hosting the CIPD HR conference; being voted one of the top 100 most influential women in the North West by Insider magazine; and winning the individual Showcase PACE Volunteer Award, which was recognition for aligning branch and CIPD strategy and raising HR's profile across the region.

Department for International Trade's Export Champion Programme

I thoroughly enjoy coaching and mentoring others and believe it is a vital opportunity to be able to give something back. With nearly twenty years' experience of working internationally I have a great deal of knowledge to share, which is why I joined the former UK Trade and Investment body (UKTI) - now the Department of International Trade (DIT) - Export Champion programme and have been an Export Champion for several years.

This programme is a business-to-business export mentorship scheme that provides companies who are new to exporting with support from companies who are experienced and successful in international markets.

Periodically, I am contacted by organizations that are new to exporting and have regular meetings with them in order to share my knowledge. Whilst mentoring others I have also found that these up and coming entrepreneurs have some very interesting business ideas and have given me insight into some new and innovative concepts.

The Institute of Directors (IoD)

The IoD is a business organization for company directors, senior business leaders and entrepreneurs. It is the UK's longest running organization for professional leaders, having been founded in 1903 and incorporated by Royal Charter in 1906.

I became a member of the IoD Northwest because I believe that if you see yourself as a leader then you should be involved with, or part of, an institute that is not only aligned to your beliefs but can also help you to develop your skills.

Working with other business leaders and entrepreneurs has helped me to grow and develop. Initially, I attended meetings and events. I spoke at the first IoD North West on Tour conference, which was held on Saturday, 25th January 2020 at the World Harvest Christian Centre, Manchester.

The event was entitled, "Women of Purpose" and was attended by 100 women from the Greater Manchester African diaspora. It was a successful event with a great line-up of speakers and the opportunity for delegates to network.

Head Judge for the IoD Awards

I have been involved in these awards for many years, attending as guest, in 2019 I was a judge for the awards and this year I had the honour of being the head judge. The annual North West & Isle of Man Director of the year awards has grown over the past 16 years to represent the pinnacle of leadership and business excellence highlighting the significant contribution business leaders can make to society and the economic prosperity in our region. Directors from diverse regional businesses have been recognised at these prestigious awards.

In 2020 the judges all came together at Kuits Solicitors' offices in Manchester, with the enormous task of judging over 100 applications, which is the highest number of applicants yet! I was joined by a brilliant panel of previous award winners, sponsors and other inspirational leaders from across the North West.

It was such a pleasure to see the sheer amount of talent and exceptional leadership that our region has to offer. In 2020 the award ceremony was held virtually, on 15th July, due to the Covid-19 pandemic and social distancing requirements. I had the pleasure of presenting an award to the winner of Director of the Year – Public Sector, Ian Hopkins, of Greater Manchester Police.

Entrepreneur Accelerator Programme and the Alison Rose Review into Female Entrepreneurship

When I opened my business in 1998 I faced many barriers, the main ones being childcare issues, mostly when the children were ill or needed collecting from school.

I did have paid childcare, however, there are times when you, as a parent, are needed and in my own experience I found it was mostly the female that had to be flexible, even though both parents were working. Other issues were access to finance and finding mentors who understood my specific business issues.

Alison Rose, CEO of Royal Bank of Scotland Group, was invited by Robert Jenrick MP, Exchequer Secretary to the Treasury at the time, to carry out a review into barriers to female entrepreneurship. They had a shared ambition to strengthen the UK's position as one of the best places in the world for women to start and grow a business. One of the outcomes of the research revealed that tailored support from specialists who understand the different challenges that female business owners face, as well as the way they think and run their business, makes a real difference to success rates. As a result of this, Alison Rose established an Entrepreneur Accelerator programme, offering fully funded support for growing businesses with ambition to scale up. Their aim is to support around 1,600 businesses through the programme in 2021.

Businesses on the Accelerator are provided with free office space in one of the bank's twelve hubs around the country, with free Wi-Fi and printing. The programme is focused on support, on the recognised barriers that entrepreneurs face, providing access to funding, new markets, infrastructure, leadership, and coaching.

In November 2019 the programme was formally endorsed by the Scale Up Institute, a not-for-profit organization which aims to make the UK "the best place in the world for SMEs to scale up". To date this programme has supported 15,000 entrepreneurs through the programme, creating nearly 1,300 jobs and contributing in excess of £103 million to the UK economy, with nearly half of the businesses supported female-led. I feel privileged to have been asked by Gemma Fattahi, Entrepreneur Development Manager and Deputy Regional Director, to join this community in my capacity as Business Mentor at the NatWest Entrepreneur Accelerator. In this role I have enjoyed working with female entrepreneurs, helping them to realise their full potential and achieve their goals.

In March 2019, I was invited to take part in a panel at the launch of the Rose Review of Female Entrepreneurship, which coincided with International Women's Day and which included Alison Rose; Robert Jenrick; Rosaleen Blair CBE, CEO of the global talent acquisition and management company Alexander Mann Solutions; and Alexandra Daly, crowdfunding consultant and author.

The panel discussion was around the "5 Key Challenges", taken from the report, that influence women's ability to start and scale up business relative to men:

1. Low access and awareness of capital – starting capital is 53% below men, only 1% of venture funding goes to all-female teams.
2. Greater risk awareness – 55% cite fear of going it alone as a primary reason.
3. Perceived missing skills & experience – only 39% of women are confident in their capabilities to start a business, compared to 55% of men.
4. Disproportionate primary care responsibilities – on average some 60% spend more time than men on primary care.
5. Lack of relatable sponsorship/mentorship/role models – 31% of women surveyed highlighted the importance of networking as a business skill, compared to 21% of men. Only 30% of women said they already knew an entrepreneur versus 38% of men.

As a female entrepreneur I had experienced these challenges myself, and whilst coaching and mentoring I had assisted other women in overcoming or mitigating them. This was a subject close to my heart and I felt I could contribute to the discussion, listening and learning from others whilst sharing my experiences and challenges with the panel and the audience.

There are three main areas of opportunity, as recommended by the report. The first is to increase funding for female entrepreneurs; secondly, to provide greater family care support for female entrepreneurs; and finally, to expand awareness and access to support, including mentorship and networking opportunities offered by existing and new networks.

Being part of this discussion and realising that a great deal of the issues I faced in 1998 were still impacting on women over twenty years later was a little disheartening. However, the recommendations and solutions are a commitment to make lasting change, and already some of these initiatives are bearing fruit. For example, from the Alison Rose review update, which was published in March 2020 there is the "Investing in Women Code", which was formally launched in 2019 and now has twenty-two signatories from the finance and investor community, and NatWest bank has announced £1 billion of ring-fenced debt funding for female-led businesses.

Marketing and Social Media

Marketing and Public Relations (PR) are key to any business success. Early on in my career working in the recruitment industry I was taught that a marketing plan is an important part of a business strategy. I remember working for Reed Employment and the excitement and pride of seeing their advert on the television, and the surge in business after a good marketing campaign, so from day one of opening my own business a strong marketing strategy was part of my plan. Initially I managed all this myself, but I knew that if I was to grow my business and be successful I needed to bring in the necessary expertise.

The purpose of a marketing agency is to identify the right campaigns, build them with you and then help you to deliver them. A good PR company should help you to enhance or build your reputation through the media. The person assigned to your organization should be able to analyse your organization, find the positive messages and translate those messages into positive media stories.

As soon as I could afford it, I employed the services of a marketing/ PR agency to help me stay connected to my current customers and to reach new customers.

In the early days, my main forms of marketing my business were by emails, leaflet drops, newspaper articles and networking - I practically attended every networking event that I could.

In later years I used radio advertising and paid for an advert on Smooth FM, ran collaborative events, advertised in the local CIPD Manchester newsletter, and provided radio interviews. Most recently I have used Podcasts, YouTube films, videos on my website, blogs and social media, mainly Facebook, LinkedIn, Twitter, and Instagram.

Finding the right marketing/PR company has proven challenging and over the past twenty years I have employed four different organizations. After lots of searching I feel I have finally found the right match for me, but each agency I have worked with has contributed to my learning and to my company's brand. The first company helped me to understand how to complete the necessary paperwork to apply for an award, and they were instrumental in helping me to win the award in 2009 for "Achievement in International Business". The second company helped with newspaper articles, Facebook, marketing materials, leaflets, stands etc. The third company helped me to rebrand OSR and create a new look for myself and then, with my new headshots, created a new by-line. We followed on with a social media campaign which greatly increased my Twitter following. They also helped me to understand how to write an engaging blog post. They were fun to work with and forward-thinking.

Over the years I have had good and bad experiences. Sometimes the person you meet initially and who represents the organization isn't the person subsequently allocated to look after your account, and this has meant some personality clashes for me. I have met someone and liked them and looked forward to working with them, and then the person I eventually got to work with was nothing like the person I connected with initially.

If the relationship is not right it can be difficult to get your vision across and for that person to then interpret your vision successfully, and ultimately the process can prove disappointing. And of course, I recognise this as a valid point to remember in my own business, as previously discussed.

Before investing in my present marketing/PR company I thought deeply about what I wanted to achieve, and my overall goal. I was looking for an organization with a proven track record of providing the specific services I was looking for.

I have a long-standing friend who is in the same industry and I remember having lunch with her; she was energised and passionate about where her business was going, having recruited new marketing/PR people. She had a new vision, had developed some new collaborative relationships, and her business was changing direction and going through a growth spurt. She recommended this company to me, but the time was not right for me then.

Some time later we met again, and I talked to her about my plans for business growth and moving in a different direction. I also shared my desire to build my presence on LinkedIn and to clarify to the business community exactly what OSR could offer. Once again, she recommended the marketing/PR company that she was using and this time I went ahead and arranged a meeting. That was nearly two years ago now and we are still working together.

We have a formal contract clarifying how we will work together, and we meet monthly to discuss our plans but speak on the phone weekly.

It is really good to work with an organization that truly understands your goal but is capable of challenging you, pushing you out of your comfort zone and coming up with new ideas about how you can grow and develop your business. My business is moving in the right direction and I am looking forward to an exciting future.

There are some key points when finding a good PR match:

1. Do your homework before recruiting a PR or marketing company. Ask for references and for permission to speak to their clients, check their track record.
2. Formalise your working relationship. You might work together for a period of time and the lines become blurred, so it is best to get clarity right at the beginning.
3. Be clear on your focus. Some companies specialise in Twitter, Instagram, or other forms of social media. I specifically wanted to build my presence on LinkedIn, for example, and not all organizations have this expertise.
4. Make sure they understand your values, your brand and your personal preferences. One company that worked for me posted a picture of a huge moustache to celebrate 'Grow a Moustache for Movember'! When I saw it on my social media feed I was horrified because I didn't think it resembled a moustache! Just to check that I wasn't overreacting I showed it to an acquaintance, who was equally horrified. I called the company and asked for the post to be taken down immediately. The PR person was not happy but ultimately it is my company and my brand. My reputation is very important to me and I will not compromise on that.
5. Check your social media feed regularly, you should be aware of how you are being portrayed at all times.

Networking is the Lifeblood of any Business

The definition of networking in the Oxford English Dictionary is: "Interact with others to exchange information and develop professional or social contacts."

Social media means that we are able to interact with others, exchange information and develop contacts using various platforms and for me this is a good starting point, but ultimately I do like to meet people face to face and make a deeper connection.

After twenty-one years of running my own business I have developed a global network. As coach, mentor, or friend, if someone asks me for a contact who can help them with a certain issue I can usually put them in touch with someone who can help them. Building a powerful network takes time and effort and, as with most things, you get out of it what you put in. But networking is a business skill that you have to work at.

From my early days of working in recruitment part of our remit was to build close working relationships with our clients. We would invite them to our events and would in return be guests at any events they were attending. What better way to build credibility with a new contact than to be introduced as a trusted supplier? Recommendation indeed, and in those days - the 1990s - we would collect business cards and then follow up with a phone call. We had to call within three days because research had shown that after three days they would not remember having met you. I remember diligently sitting down with all my business cards and calling everyone before those three days had expired!

I knew how important it was to network in the early days of establishing OSR and I attended every networking group that I could. I wanted to spread the word about my business and meet new contacts that could help me to grow. Some I enjoyed, some I would walk away from thinking, "Well that was a complete waste of my time!"

I decided that in order to get the best out of networking I would attend some seminars so I could understand the do's and don't's. One of the key things I learned was to be discerning about which networking events to attend. Ask the organiser for a list of attendees ahead of the event to make sure that the people in the room are your target audience.

There is nothing more frustrating than attending an event when you realise that everyone is working in the same field as yourself. If you have driven a long way, paid for parking and are wearing your best suit, you feel justifiably frustrated, so do your homework first.

Being an entrepreneur can be lonely. When you have a team of staff you cannot always share your concerns and anxieties with them because it is important that they feel positive, motivated, and focused on your business. You may have a family, or a partner, but they don't always want you to come home every night and unload all your problems on them. This can be unfair and in the long term could damage your relationships, so having a network of people who are going through the same experience as you, or have been through it, is extremely beneficial.

Before attending a networking event, decide if you are going for business purposes or for professional development. Sometimes an event can achieve both, but I do have a different mindset depending on which one I am attending. For business networking I ask key questions before confirming my attendance:

1. What is the theme or purpose of the event?
2. Who is the speaker and what is the subject matter?
3. How many are attending? This can vary, depending on where the event is being held and the weather. It is normal for most events to have at least a 20% - 50% drop out rate, particularly if it's free.
4. Are you seated at a table or mingling around? If at a table, who is sitting at your table, because depending on timing you may have limited opportunity to meet other attendees? If you are going to be sitting cabaret style at a table, it is useful to know the background of your companion. Having a look at LinkedIn and doing some research will help as a conversation starter.
5. With the present situation regarding social distancing we have had to find new ways of networking, via Zoom, Microsoft teams, to name a few. Booking our places on

events takes place through systems such as Eventbrite, however, there is normally details of the organiser and contact details if required. It is still possible to ring them and ask some pertinent questions before committing your time.

6. A question I always pose to myself is, "Why am I going to this event, what is my goal in attending?"

One of my most recent experiences of how powerful networking can be was during a visit to Dominica last year, where I met a friend of my sister, Liza, who worked for many years in the legal profession in the UK but emigrated to the Caribbean. One evening she invited me to a network meeting of professional women of which she was a part. It was very informal but good fun, and there were approximately twelve very interesting women there. During the evening I made a new connection and we continued to keep in contact via LinkedIn.

A few months later, I was back in the UK when I received an enquiry regarding an event that was being organised for the following year. I had been recommended by my new connection in Dominica. The upshot of this was that through attending this networking meeting in August 2019, I was invited to be the Keynote Speaker at an event called "Inspiring Ladies of the Caribbean" in March 2020, in Curaçao - where I made many more contacts, some of which I am now planning future projects with.

Every year I attend the Women of the Year UK Award Ceremony as a guest of my lovely friend Emma Elston. I met Emma for the first time at a NatWest event in 2015 that was held for women in business.

Emma was the guest speaker and had just been awarded the MBE. She is the co-founder and CEO of UK Container Maintenance Ltd but she also has many more business interests and is a real entrepreneur. Since meeting Emma five years ago we have kept in touch with each other.

She is one of the most kind and generous people I have ever met. She has used my services as a consultant to work in her businesses on more than one occasion and has taken a personal interest in my success. For the past three years Emma has invited me to join her at the Women of the Year award as her guest at her table. Most recently it was Emma's suggestion that I become an Ambassador for the Woman of the Year Award. I feel like Emma has my best interests at heart and is always looking for opportunities to help me to thrive. She is remarkable because everyone I speak to who has had the privilege of meeting her also remarks about her generosity of spirit and ability to nurture others, as well as her sharp business acumen.

The Women of the Year Award is always held in a beautiful venue, the room is stylishly arranged and there is wonderful entertainment. I attend this event for my own personal development because I love listening to the stories of the women who win the award and I always learn something new. I have met some incredible women and heard stories of remarkable courage. One year I met Dr. Helen Pankhurst, activist and granddaughter of Sylvia, great-granddaughter of Emmeline Pankhurst. Having studied Emmeline Pankhurst and the Suffragette Movement at school it was fabulous to meet one of her descendants.

At the Women of the Year Award the main opportunity to network takes place whilst you are sitting at your table and one year I was fortunate enough to sit next to Dr. Baroness Newlove; we made a connection and chatted through lunch. I had heard Helen's story via the television news and the press, when she suffered the terrible tragedy of her husband's murder. I had always admired her from afar; she is so resilient, turning something that could have destroyed her life into a cause for good.

We subsequently connected on social media, Twitter, and Linked In, and one day Helen arranged for me to have lunch with her at the House of Lords.

I have visited many historical buildings over the years but I never thought I would have the opportunity to visit the House of Lords, with its rich and interesting history. It was a wonderful experience and Helen was a fabulous host, taking the time to give me a tour. We continue to keep in touch, she is a great support.

Networking has been a big part of my success as a businesswoman so I encourage everyone to take the opportunity to get out there, you never know where it might lead! My key tips for networking are:

N – Nurture your contacts; understand their needs and where you can support. I don't believe in just taking, it's important to give back. I always say to people, "You have taken the time to do something for me, what can I do for you?" It's a two-way street. A lot of people say, it's okay I want to do this for you, I just want to help you. I must say that over the years I am always blown away by how many people have shown me kindness and consideration. I am blessed with many wonderful people in my life.

E – Empathise. Everyone is going through their own personal challenges; I always say to myself, "Olive, it's not just about you!" Often people will reach out to you, suggesting you meet for coffee or a chat and you can't say yes every time, but I try to understand their mood and give them what they need. Sometimes it's just a listening ear, or advice. I try to give time to my contacts when they need me.

T – Time. Investing time in people that are important to you is vital. You might meet someone on your travels who could be of value to one of your networks. Take the time to make the connection and facilitate introductions. Sharing a contact with another person for their benefit enriches both of you.

W – Work. Preserving your network means you have to work at it. Sometimes my contacts are hosting an event and need to fill some places and will ask me to help them, or I might be asked to speak at an event for them pro bono. I always try to give something back.

Over the years I have had a lot of support from various people who know they can call upon me for help if they need it.

O – Open. Be open to opportunities and new ideas. When people meet you for the first time, they may spot a talent you have not exploited, or have an idea that you had not thought of. By networking I often leave excited and refreshed by that person's clarity of vision, or creative idea that I can put to good use.

R – Reflect. Take time to reflect on who is in your network, and when you are setting your goals think about the people you are spending time with. If you want to move to the next level in your professional life do you need to expand your network, or reach out to different types of people? For example, when I received more demand to work with CEO's and board directors I made enquiries about joining a network called Women on Boards (WOB), which is a network of experienced senior leaders and serving non-executives who are there to support women in their boardroom aspirations, focused on helping women get to the top in all sectors.

K – Knowledge. Share your knowledge with your network either through mentoring, coaching or just facilitating meetings. I specialise in consultancy and the learning and development industry. Often, I will get a phone call from an old contact who will ask to meet for coffee or lunch. They would like to discuss a problem or issue they are having and ask for my advice on the best way to deal with it. Once again, I may not always be available, but when I can I either meet or have a discussion on the phone.

CHAPTER 11

BEING CREDIBLE

Having been in business for over twenty-one years there are some suppliers who have been with me for a long time, and others with whom I have had shorter term relationships. One of my suppliers has been with me for over eleven years, providing me with IT support. Our relationship has persisted because they are trustworthy, and I recommend them to all my friends and clients. When I have a problem, no matter where I am in the world, they come to the rescue, making sure that I have all I need to continue working. Our relationship has evolved from them helping me out with PC basics to using cloud-based software and even helping me with my mobile phone, as it is linked to my laptop and PC. They give a consistent and professional service; they are competent, sincere and loyal. This is what I look for when I work closely with an organization. This is also what I offer to my clients, being trustworthy, ethical, knowledgeable and professional.

Being Competent through Qualifications

The main selling point for me is competence, and I have always strived to demonstrate that my company is competent. This cannot be taken for granted and part of me proving that my business is credible is offering clients my professional knowledge of learning and development, specialising in leadership and management development, female entrepreneurship, and diversity and inclusion. I work closely with my clients: Board Directors, Human Resource professionals, managers, and leaders. OSR offers bespoke packages where we look at an organization's business plan and ensure that our training programmes are aligned to the organization's strategy. We also weave company policies, values, mission and goals together with the culture so that our solutions are aligned with the organization's overall goals.

My work takes me all over the world and it is important that I remain credible. My qualifications (a Postgraduate Diploma in Human Resource Management and a Master's Degree in Human Resource Management) demonstrate to current and potential clients that I understand my profession. I am a Chartered Fellow of the CIPD, so I have access to up-to-date research within my profession. For my international work, I have international clients and work closely with the DIT, once again ensuring that I am up to date with international developments. I am a Member of the Institute of Directors and the European Mentoring and Coaching Council (EMCC). However, I cannot rest on my laurels. I believe it's essential that I keep my knowledge current, which means developing myself so I can offer my clients that something extra.

Being Competent through Increasing Knowledge

Every year the CIPD holds a three-day event called the Annual Conference and Exhibition (ACE), at Manchester Central Conference Centre. Human Resource and training and development professionals come together here from all over the world to take the opportunity to keep up to date with any new developments in the learning arena. They can talk to suppliers of books, games and resources, listen to keynote speakers and attend workshops held by influencers in the training and development market. Attending this event ensures that you are seen by your clients and prospective clients and you keep abreast of any innovative and creative ideas that could add to your offering to clients.

In addition to attending conferences and events in the UK, I also work on building my credibility internationally. In 2014 I joined a trade mission organised by the DIT (UKTI) to Barbados and Trinidad and Tobago. The purpose of this was to understand the Caribbean learning and development market and to make some relevant contacts.

The DIT has representatives in these countries and plans the event and sends out an itinerary outlining activities whilst you are there. At the trade fair in Trinidad and Tobago I was offered some work and met some great contacts, which I have maintained.

One of these contacts has become a dear friend and my husband and I attended their wedding on a beach in Barbados. The list of contacts that I met during this trade mission is part of a Caribbean database that I am compiling. I keep in touch via LinkedIn and send them regular emails together with my newsletter to keep me in the forefront of their minds. Attending this trade mission was extremely informative, with many business presentations and informative data regarding the Caribbean economy and their current and future requirements for learning and development.

When you work for yourself it can be easy to neglect your own personal development. I do attend events around business strategy, leadership development etc, locally and nationally. However, as I want to build an international business, expanding my knowledge through travel and attending global events are all part of my plan. I see attending global events as having many benefits, not only increasing my knowledge of the business world but increasing my professional resilience.

At the end of November 2016, I managed to tick off an item on my bucket list, as well as increase my development. I attended GoPRO 2016 at the Las Vegas Convention Centre in Nevada. I have always wanted to visit Las Vegas and see the Grand Canyon, so prior to attending the conference I took the opportunity to do some sightseeing. I boarded a small plane and flew over the Mohave Desert, the Hoover Dam and the Grand Canyon, where we stopped for a picnic lunch. It was an extremely memorable experience, especially walking across the Skywalk – a ten-foot-wide, horseshoe-shaped glass bridge, which extends seventy feet out over the rim of the Grand Canyon. If you look down you can see right through the glass platform, 4,000 feet to the floor of the canyon below. After that breath-taking experience I felt ready to tackle anything and arrived at the GoPRO event ready to absorb, learn, and participate.

There was an interesting array of speakers including Eric Worre, American author and leading authority on coaching network marketing professionals; John Addison, American CEO of the Addison Leadership Group; Mel Robbins, American TV host, author and motivational speaker; Sir Richard Branson, British business magnate, investor and author and founder of the Virgin Group; and Tony Robbins, American author, public speaker, life coach and philanthropist. I firmly believe that to achieve success you need to model someone who is already doing what you want to achieve or, in the words of Anthony Robbins, "The key to success? Model the best." Being in the room with some great speakers and successful entrepreneurs, along with 20,000 people, was extremely motivational. When I left the event after three days, I felt energised, positive, focused, and with a written plan for the coming year.

In July 2019 I attended the 25th anniversary of the ESSENCE Festival in New Orleans, run by ESSENCE, the number one media, technology and commerce company serving Black women in the USA. It was an incredible experience organised for me by my friend Dijonn Taylor, CEO and founder of Savvy Guest. The "ESSENCE Fest" as it is locally referred to, is the largest African-American culture and music event in the United States and on this anniversary attracted more than half a million people. The ESSENCE Chief Executive Officer, Michelle Ebanks, said, "The 25th anniversary Essence Festival represented a truly transformative global homecoming celebration for Black women and the Black community. This year's extraordinary turnout reflects ESSENCE's uniquely powerful engagement of Black women around personal empowerment, community, and culture."

It was one of the most memorable experiences of my life. There were live broadcasts called 'Presidential spotlight' and "candidate conversations", which were on television stations MSNBC and CNN, with keynote speakers Senators Cory Booker, Kamala Harris, and Elizabeth Warren, and the Reverend Al Sharpton, American civil rights activist, Baptist minister, talk show host and politician.

Over 100 artists performed, including Mary J. Blige, Missy Elliott, Pharrell Williams and Patti LaBelle. There were more than 300 influencers, leaders, and creators such as Ava Duvernay, film producer of "When They See Us"; actor Tyler Perry; Congresswoman Maxine Waters; businesswoman and former senior advisor to President Barack Obama, Valerie Jarrett; model, actress and entrepreneur, Iman; and the brilliant Iyanla Vanzant, an American inspirational speaker, lawyer, New Thought spiritual teacher, author, life coach and television personality, among many others. But for me, the highlight of the festival was seeing Michelle Obama, who took to the stage at the sold-out superdome on 7th July, 2019. After reading Michelle Obama's book, "Becoming", my respect for her grew. In her book she shares with us the story of her upbringing, her values and her contribution to Barack Obama's election as President, in addition to the challenges she faced from the press in America, the horrific insulting headlines, and the abuse she had to contend with. Through it all, she built an incredible team around her, brought up two children and maintained a good marriage. She is also working hard into putting something back by championing good causes around the world. She is beautiful, strong, intelligent and an example to us all. I sat there listening to this amazing woman, totally transfixed by her.

Having seen New Orleans for many years on screen and in films I was eager to take some time to explore during my stay. I wanted to experience everything, from travelling down the Mississippi River to going to a plantation house, even touching a live alligator whilst visiting the swamps!

I returned to the UK with a feeling of extreme joy, renewal and feeling tremendously empowered to move forward in my business in a different way.

I often share my experiences of travelling abroad and how important it is to invest in your own learning when I deliver motivational speeches.

CHAPTER 12

DIVERSITY AND INCLUSION

"Every person, regardless of their ethnicity or background, should be able to fulfil their potential at work. That is the business case as well as the moral case. Diverse organizations that attract and develop individuals from the widest pool of talent consistently perform better."

Race in the Workplace – The McGregor-Smith Review, February 2017

In light of what has happened recently with the Black Lives Matter movement, I thought I would share my experiences of racism, its impact on me and how I have dealt with it, both in my professional life and my personal life.

As a Black professional who has lived in the UK since 1968, I welcomed this report as I recognised there was a need to focus on and nurture Black talent.

I arrived in the UK when I was six years old, and grew up in Blackburn, Lancashire. My sister and I were the only Black children in the school we attended. It was extremely challenging being the only two amongst so many people.

One of my early memories around diversity and equality was being accused of stealing. My mother believes that cleanliness is next to Godliness and wanted her four daughters to look and smell nice, so every morning after our wash she would make us put on a roll-on antiperspirant.

One day I was at school chatting to some friends and the teacher, who was rather young, walked past me and said, "You smell nice, what have you got on?" I replied that it was antiperspirant, and she then said that she had dropped her perfume and someone had stolen it, and that whatever I was wearing had a similar fragrance to the perfume that had been stolen.

I was mortified to be accused of such a thing in front of my classmates. She asked if I lived locally, which I did, and I was sent home to get what I was wearing to bring as evidence that I had not stolen her perfume. So off I went home. My father worked nights so was asleep when I knocked on the door, and he was absolutely furious. When I explained why I had come home in the middle of a school day, he took my hand and walked me back to school so fast that I had to run to keep up with him. I don't know what was said but I heard a lot of shouting between my father, the head teacher Sister Mary Magdalene, and the teacher who had accused me. After that day I never saw that teacher again. It is something that I never forgot; the embarrassment of being singled out, everyone staring, being sent home, and all for something of which I was not guilty.

I have lived in the UK for the majority of my life, and have always felt like I stood out, which obviously I do. The education system at the time fed into my feelings of insecurity and feeling different because, for example, when studying history at school we talked about the Kings and Queens of England, which was very interesting, but when I asked my teacher about my history as a Black person he showed me a picture of a slave ship, with people lying down packed in like sardines, and said, "That is your history, you came over on the slave ships." And that was that. I shrunk down into my seat feeling terrible. Was that it? Was there nothing good or positive about my history to share?

All around me there were no positive images of Black people. The films on television showed us speaking in a slow, southern, unintelligible drawl, rolling our eyes and grinning. In the war films the Black guy always sacrificed himself and got killed right at the beginning. Things slowly began to improve when Trevor McDonald and Moira Stewart arrived to present the news on television, and Sir Clive Lloyd became a famous cricketer.

I remember my father going into work with real confidence when the West Indies won at cricket - something to be proud of!

We would sit around the television as a family, bursting with pride to see Trevor and Moira - someone who looked like us - not doing a menial task, but speaking with authority. It was great!

As I child I truly thought that Black people were insignificant, because that was all I saw around me. I thought my history started when we were put on a slave ship and that we only had menial jobs and did nothing else. In order to build my self-worth and confidence, I needed to see people like me as leaders, being listened to and being able to influence others. That is why I advocate role models that reflect the ethnic origins of the population, because in this way the person grows and develops with some pride and self-esteem.

When I was twelve years old, I was watching television when something miraculous happened. The BBC was showing a film about Martin Luther King Jr., the American civil rights activist. During the *March on Washington for Jobs and Freedom* on 28th August 1963, he called for civic and economic rights and an end to racism in the United States in his now famous "I have a dream" speech. I sat there transfixed at this Black man who spoke so eloquently; his beautiful voice, so melodious; the passion behind his words; the evocative use of language. I was filled with pride and admiration; my chest filled out and my head came up. Yes! Here was someone who was Black like me, someone I could admire, and who commanded such respect from others.

From that day onwards I stood a little straighter and walked with an extra spring in my step, I had someone who I could hold up and aspire to. Later on, I was able to add Nelson Mandela to my list, along with Maya Angelou and more recently, Barack and Michelle Obama.

Before opening my business, I was employed by a variety of organizations, some of which would single me out when they were looking at figures for diversity, or to achieve awards. Normally I would never be asked to attend any meetings with senior management, but I remember a few occasions when I would be called into a meeting with my manager present, to be asked how was I treated?

Did I ever experience any racist behaviour and how happy was I with the way I was managed?

Of course, I would say everything was fine and they would tick the appropriate box. They had proven that they had a Black employee. I was often the token Black, which is why I do not like tokenism when it comes to diversity and inclusion.

As a result of my own early experiences, I wanted to ensure that my children - and now grandchildren - did not feel the way I did growing up. I wanted them to have positive role models and to grow up with confidence and a sense of pride. Both my husband and I work for ourselves and we have always involved our children in our businesses from an early age. Errol also used to take the children to different initiatives such as "Bring your child to work day", so they could get a feel for different work environments. We wanted to immerse our children in the professional business world and encourage them to have high aspirations.

I feel as a Black female entrepreneur I am well placed to use my knowledge and experience to influence others. With this in mind I seek opportunities where I can embrace any business projects which give me the chance to get involved with diversity and inclusion.

I joined the Ethnic Minority Business Forum North West (EMBFNW) and was part of its first awards ceremony in 2009, recognising and rewarding the huge contribution that Black, Asian and minority ethnic (BAME) individuals and businesses make to the regional economy. I have delivered training and been a speaker for the National Black Police Association (NBPA). Charles Critchlow, the past president, has been a great support to me. I coach and mentor others and often speak at events around diversity and inclusion, where I share my story.

When I was awarded the MBE, I announced it on my social media channels, including Twitter, and Peter Cheese, the CEO of the CIPD tweeted the following: "Many congratulations Olive! Well-deserved as a great role model and advocate for great people management and inclusion."

Seeing this Tweet gave me an immense sense of achievement because it meant that my goal to champion inclusion, diversity and management was being recognised by others.

Why is it important to have Diversity in the Boardroom?
During the twenty-one years of working for myself I have worked all over the world and met with many senior managers, board directors and CEO's but I can honestly say that out of all the organizations I have worked for in the UK, I have only met two CEO's that are BAME, one Asian man and one Black one. The Boards are the mind and will of a company, and they perform better when they include the best people coming from a range of backgrounds and perspectives. There is a lot of research that proves the business case for diversity and inclusion, including well respected organizations such as McKinsey, KPMG and Deloitte. The boardroom is where all strategic decisions are made, risk overseen, and governance applied. Diversity encompasses age, ethnicity, gender, LGBT, but also diversity of skills, competencies, philosophies, and life experiences.

Data to prove the Business Case for Diverse Boards

The Hampton Alexander Report, produced and now backed by the UK Government, specialises in looking at specific areas and making recommendations with a view to achieving greater gender parity and diversity on boards.

Jill Treanor of The Guardian newspaper reported, "Measures introduced after a review finds that only 85 of 1,050 directors in FTSE 100 companies are from ethnic minorities."

Sir John Parker, the chairman of the mining company Anglo American, who conducted the review, said that it should be a wake-up call for major companies. The companies in the FTSE 100 have been told to end their all-white boardrooms by 2021, while those in FTSE 250 have until 2024. The target is voluntary but companies failing to comply will have to explain why.

Business Case for Diversity

Sir John Parker, who led the review, said "The boardrooms of Britain's leading companies do not reflect the ethnic diversity of either the UK or the stakeholders that they seek to engage and represent."

Ethnic minority representation in the boardrooms across the FTSE 100 and 250 is disproportionately low and at the time of writing this, spring 2020, the news is that we are regressing, and top firms are still failing to recruit ethnic minority directors. One of the reasons given for this is that they do not know how to source BAME staff.

Challenges we need to Overcome

Avoid the merit trap. Be careful of using the meritocracy and recruiting in our own shadows. And avoid tokenism – just because we have one BAME person, we can't say that we are done!
- Educate ourselves around unconscious bias.
- Embrace different personalities, cultures and beliefs.
- Directors feel uncomfortable, do not have friends or contacts who are minorities and therefore do not know how to address a Black person and are not sure how to start a conversation.

We have been conditioned - when you think of influence and power, is it mainly a white man you think of? We must challenge ourselves.

Research completed by the CIPD states that 34% of British people do not have a friend with a BAME background, so the chances of the board recruiting someone with whom they do not feel comfortable is limited.

My business involves working with organizations and board directors around leadership, vision, values, and culture. I always take the opportunity to discuss diversity and inclusion and how to make boards more diverse.

Looking at things like their talent pipeline, cultural barriers and monitoring the diversity profile of their workforce at all levels, including senior managers and board level. In order to make a diverse boardroom not just an initiative but part of the DNA of the business, it needs to be linked to values and beliefs, and senior management need to model the appropriate behaviour.

On 25th May 2020, George Floyd, a 46-year-old Black man, was killed in Minneapolis. This sparked an international outcry with global condemnation of this, and hundreds of protests not just in America, but all around the world.

In the UK the CIPD is developing and creating practical content on their hub to help members and people professionals tackle racism. I have been involved in two webinars called "Conversations on Race" with the IoD North West Online, organised by Claire Ebrey, Regional Director – North West, and hosted by Sharon Amesu and Marilyn Comrie OBE. These webinars discussed the way forward and proposed solutions to tackling racism and making lasting change. Similarly, I have been involved in a BAME + Allies Power Circle organised by Simone Roche MBE of Northern Power Women, again focusing on what we can do to increase understanding of racism, recognise its impact and galvanise and influence positive change.

From a business point of view, I have seen increased requests for racial equality and anti-racism training, in order to help organizations build diverse and supportive cultures of respect and fairness for all.

We can help organizations to address the importance of a diversity and inclusion strategy that includes a focus on racial equality. I have worked with many organizations to achieve this over the past twenty years and I relish the prospect of continuing to do so.

CHAPTER 13

MENTORING AND COACHING
AND PROVIDING SUPPORT

"Mentoring is a long-term process based on mutual trust and respect. Coaching, on the other hand, is for a short period of time. Mentoring is more focused on creating an informal association between the mentor and mentee, whereas coaching follows a more structured and formal approach."

Definition from European Mentoring & Coaching Council (EMCC)

Looking back at my life, my first mentors were my parents. My mother taught me to be dignified, have respect for myself and others and take a pride in my appearance. Presentation was always important to my Mum. My father was an entrepreneur. He established two businesses in the Caribbean during his lifetime, a grocer shop and a bakery, and my mother took care of the books and ensured they remained solvent. My father was the salesman, extremely charismatic and engaging.

My first business mentors were people I met whilst I was working in recruitment, at Reed Employment. Collette Gordon, who ran the temporary staff division, and Rita Logan, who was in charge of the permanent division, both took me under their wings and helped me to hit the ground running. They not only paved the way for me by giving me good advice but also introduced me to clients and gave me assistance when I made mistakes. One of my first coaches was Cathy Martin, my manager at Reed Employment. She was a hard taskmaster and the 1980s were difficult times, but Cathy continued to coach me, recognised my potential and gave me the opportunity to grow and develop, eventually promoting me into a management position.

To establish, grow and sustain a business for over twenty years you need support, mentoring and coaching. I am lucky to have some wonderful people in my life who have been there for me at crucial times. Owning your own business can be extremely lonely because although you can canvass opinion and ask for someone else's input, ultimately the buck stops with you. You have to make the final decision and live with the consequences; others can walk away but you can't.

My husband, Errol, and our children have been very supportive over the years. Errol was the company accountant for the first year and both children have worked in the business at various times. My daughter, Rhia Boyode, who is also a qualified HR professional, provided HR support, creating policies and procedures and at one time ran the office for me, looking after our staff, preparing contracts for our freelance consultants and allocating work to them, freeing me up to focus on building the global business.

My son, Ricky, has also been involved in working for OSR and his role was client-focused, dealing with sales and marketing. Both my children gained experience from working for OSR and the business has also benefited from their input, each bringing their particular expertise to bear. My daughter is now an HR Director and my son left to work for the Stock Exchange and still works in the finance industry. They are both very intelligent, capable individuals and I am extremely proud of both of them.

Over the years my business has thrived but has also suffered during the recession, most recently with the Covid-19 pandemic. This has meant that my contribution to the household has not always been constant and sometimes we have had to use our savings to keep things afloat, or my husband has had to make additional contributions to see me through, so my family are a big part of my story and have contributed to my success.

At the start of my business journey I received some free mentoring from Business Link, a government-funded business advice and guidance service in England which sadly ceased operations in 2012. I was allocated a lovely man called David as my mentor. I received advice on how to put together a business plan and where to open a business account to get the best deal possible. I also received a small grant which came in very handy in the early days. David's mentoring was very useful; I knew what I wanted to achieve in establishing my business but David's mentoring helped me to see the possible pitfalls and to avoid mistakes that could have had an impact on my success. He advised me to open an account with the NatWest, who allocated a business manager to my account.

Having good financial advice is something that I value and is essential to a sustainable business. During the twenty years with NatWest I have had three business managers but the one that I feel has had the most long-term impact on me and my business is Gemma Fattahi. She is no longer my manager but is now Entrepreneur Development Manager/Deputy Regional Director North. Over the years she has given me great business advice but also invited me to business networking events and supported any events I have held. I have also been invited to speak at NatWest events because of Gemma's recommendation. I see her as coach/mentor and friend.

As an Export Champion I offer mentoring services to organizations wanting to work internationally. I have also received mentoring from the DIT. There is a rich vein of knowledge there and you can access mentoring for most exporting markets. Bobbie Charleston-Price, who is the International Trade Team Leader, has been working with me for many years, offering excellent coaching in exporting. She would help and support me and when necessary would refer me to the wider team to help with other aspects of establishing and growing a global business.

Bev Mullin, Deputy Head of UK Regions – North West, has also taken an interest in supporting and guiding me to achieve success globally.

When you have a question or a concern and you are able to tap into the expertise required, it really helps with your confidence and increases your knowledge.

I have had many unofficial mentors, too, mainly friends who have either business knowledge or industry expertise, who answered my phone calls, or met me for lunch or coffee, and just listened to me and shared the benefit of their experience with me. There have been many times in my life when I have reached out to my girlfriends and they have been there for me, to commiserate with me during the hard times but also to help celebrate my success. For example, not only did I have a fabulous celebration at the Ritz with my family when I received the MBE, I was also very touched because three separate sets of friends arranged three surprise parties for me! They have all been part of my journey and it was lovely to celebrate together.

I would say that it is very important to have a good mentor, you can't do it alone. Once you are clear on what you want to do, find someone who has the knowledge or skill set that you lack, or aspire to, and ask them to mentor you. I have been turned down a few times, but I have also been fortunate to receive good mentoring.

When I first opened OSR in 1998, coaching was not as popular as it is now; it tended to be only very rich people, such as Richard Branson, who had their own personal coach. Gradually this changed and I received more and more requests to provide coaching for managers and leaders. I am always asked, when I deliver presentations about my story, who coached me? As a business professional I have paid for coaching in the past and at one point, when my life was particularly challenging, I invested in some counselling.

I have always chosen my coaches carefully, usually investing in someone who has a particular skill and knowledge that I need to grow and develop my business, or someone who understands me and is able to challenge and stretch me to the next level.

My most recent business coach has proven to be a good investment for me and my business, helping me to move in a new direction.

Over the years I have coached many individuals, some senior management, using 360 degree feedback analysis to assess their areas for development, some to improve their skills and grow their potential, others with business coaching for business owners who want to improve their abilities. I have coached internationally using SKYPE and because of the time difference it has meant getting up at 7am. I understand the benefits of coaching and over the years have invested in coaching for myself. Finding the right coach can be challenging, so I prefer to choose one who has been recommended by others and has a history of dealing with the situations that I am facing. Personality is important, too, I am an individual and I want someone who I enjoy working with and who understands me.

CHAPTER 14

LEAVING A LEGACY

I have achieved so many goals in my life that I am proud of, but I never dreamed of being awarded the MBE for my contribution to Exports and to Professional Business Services.

When I received the letter asking would I accept the award if I were to receive it, I thought someone was pulling my leg because I had no indication that this would happen! I rang my daughter to tell her about it, thinking she would tell me it was some sort of scam and to just ignore it but instead she said, "Oh yes, I know about this!" She had been contacted the previous year and informed that I was being considered for an award, and although they did not say what the award was they needed certain details and contacts from her in order to do the necessary paperwork. It was an amazing moment to realise that this was authentic.

Thursday, 7th February 2019, was the day of the investiture at Buckingham Palace. It was absolutely marvellous! Errol, Rhia and Ricky all came with me to the ceremony, whilst my son-in-law Tony and my son's fiancée Serayna and granddaughters Zendaya, Sophia and Ezrah met us afterwards at the palace gates. The one person missing was my granddaughter Mya, who wasn't able to come.

More than eighty people were receiving various awards that day and whilst we were waiting to receive our awards from Prince Charles we were able to network with each other. We were understandably very nervous. However, everyone involved in the Investiture Ceremony works very hard to make each and every person feel welcome; they are concerned that you and your family are okay and make the whole experience magical. It is a very emotional moment when your name is called out and you are aware of your family sitting in the audience, it is a shared experience. They were aware of all the challenges I had been through to get to this moment, and they have been part of my story, through the good times and the bad.

I received my award from Prince Charles, who said a few words to me and was somehow able to make me feel like I was the most important person in the room. I know it takes years of training, but I was completely overawed by the whole experience.

After leaving the Palace, my family and I went for lunch at the Ritz, organised by my lovely daughter, Rhia, who also booked our travel and accommodation. Sitting around the table with my family, celebrating this most auspicious occasion, made the day even more perfect, if that were possible!

Being awarded the MBE has been one of the crowning glories of my life. Sadly, my father did not live to see this happen, however, my mother, who still lives in Dominica in the Caribbean, is inordinately proud of me. I have visited her and shown her the video of my ceremony and she was so moved, she just wanted to watch it over and over again. I also have three sisters, Liza, Susan and Sharon, who are also very proud.

I have two children and four grandchildren. My children have both achieved professional success and are bringing up their children with a strong work ethic. I want my grandchildren to see me as a yardstick, but also to know that there is no limitation on their success.

On days when I feel imposter syndrome taking over, or think about the many things that I have not achieved, I look at my MBE and remember that sense of accomplishment!

CHAPTER 15

SELF-BELIEF AND POSITIVITY

My journey has not always been plain sailing and there have been times when I have been plagued with self-doubt. Developing a deep-seated belief that "I can" has been crucial in enabling me to ride out the rough times. So how do I remain positive and driven?

Emotional Intelligence

Part of being emotionally intelligent is being self-aware, understanding myself and my feelings, knowing my strengths and weaknesses, being self-confident and having faith in myself. Over the years I have taken time to reflect on and evaluate my success and where I have struggled and why. This introspection has helped me to focus on what I do best and not try to be something that I am not, in other words, to be authentic. When you try to fit in and follow others, rather than being your authentic self, you are constantly disappointed and question yourself all the time. But when you accept yourself by celebrating your good points and accepting your bad, life is much more rewarding.

Emotional Health

If I was to analyse myself, I would say that I am emotionally strong and both friends and clients call me when they are in need of a dose of positivity and fun. I usually wake up in the morning glad to be alive and looking forward to what the day holds for me. But during my years in business there was a time when I found it hard to be my normal, ebullient self.

I was experiencing family challenges, my husband was working away, and the training market was going through the doldrums. I felt that I was being hit from all sides and not able to face life with my usual optimism.

Every time I met a friend, I would be complaining about something and I felt I was being unfair to them. I decided to get some counselling and asked for recommendations from a friend.

I met with my counsellor, we completed all the necessary paperwork, agreed we could work together and arranged our first hourly session. I launched into my many concerns and spoke for sixty minutes, pouring everything out. When I finally paused for breath, my therapist asked, picking up on my final point, "So how did that make you feel?" I looked at her and said, "Don't answer my question with a question, what do you think about what I have just told you?" She replied that therapy was not about her giving me the answers but allowing me to gain better understanding of my issues through good questioning and probing techniques. I told her, "I don't want that, I am asking you to tell me what you think?" and in response to my request she said, "Olive, do you think you are the only one?" For me that was the moment of truth. I sat back and thought about what she had said. All my perceived problems were no worse than anyone else's. I had allowed things to grow out of proportion and needed to find some solutions. That was an extremely powerful and useful meeting and for me it turned everything around.

I am sharing this experience because as a professional speaker I often share my story with the audience and more and more I am asked questions about my mental and emotional health and how I take care of myself. People in the audience often admit that they are seeing a therapist, almost as though they are ashamed of it. My reply is that self-care is about knowing yourself and understanding your needs. It is important to identify what you are feeling and get the appropriate support. There will be times when you need a mentor or coach, and times when therapy is the best thing. Get the help you need when you need it.

Goal Setting

Part of knowing and understanding yourself is working out how to get the best from your abilities.

I love goals and challenges, they are what drive me as a person! I start the year by setting my goals, I say them out loud and I write them down. Committing them to paper means that I have a plan and as I achieve my goals, I tick them off my list. I also love a full calendar and diary; it gives me a sense of purpose and things to look forward to. That's why, when the Covid-19 pandemic became a reality and all my face to face training was cancelled for the following three months, I felt devastated. In previous crises I was able to look to international markets for potential work but as the whole world was experiencing the same problem, I could not see a way forward.

However, as lockdown was extended, I realised that I had to create a new plan for myself and set daily goals to get me through this situation. I focused on keeping healthy, cooking food from scratch with good nutritional value and taking lots of exercise which included walking and following YouTube exercise videos.

I believe in setting yourself goals, writing them down, and sticking to them so you have something to focus on, and then you can reward yourself when you achieve them!

Neuroscience

I believe in having a powerful vision. When you visualise something, for example, delivering a successful presentation, you go there and go through it in your mind. Neural circuits in the brain are activated so that when you are in the live situation you find it easier and more relaxing to deliver the actual presentation.

Visualisation creates new neural pathways and can refine, deepen and strengthen existing ones.
The neuroscience of visualisation is a technique whereby you actively focus your attention on creating an image of a future goal, or outcome, or scenario. I use visualisation techniques a lot in my work, but I make sure that I focus on what I want, and not what I don't want!

Associate with Positive People

I select my friends and acquaintances carefully, which may seem harsh but people who are constantly negative and spend most of their time trying to chip away at my self-esteem and ridicule my dreams and aspirations are not part of my circle of friends. Life is hard enough without having people who are close to you trying to sabotage your efforts. I would prefer to have a few people who believe in me, challenge me, push me to be the best I can be, than a lot of people who don't really like me but are there because they perceive me to be someone who is useful or good to be around. There have been instances in my professional and personal life when I have come across people who have been unpleasant to me, or tried to shake my confidence in myself, and when it happens I would say to myself, "I'm being overly sensitive, they did not mean it the way it sounded, I shouldn't take it personally."

There is a saying by Maya Angelou, "When people show you who they are, believe them." When I was younger, I gave people second and third chances and forgave so many times. These days I take time to observe people, listen to them and examine their behaviour. If, after my analysis, I feel that having them around me brings me more misery than joy, I distance myself from them, avoiding contact where possible. Life is too short to be with people who make you unhappy.

CHAPTER 16

MAKING TIME FOR YOU

Self Care

Self-care is about taking care of your mental, emotional and physical health. In the early days of running my business I must admit that I did not put this very high on my list. I was building a business and driven to succeed. Every day I focused on my goal and every evening I would review what I had achieved, then make a fresh list for the following day with improvements so that I could do better. In the early days my main thoughts were about maintaining my stamina.

Starting my own company was my big chance in life, I was fulfilling my dreams. I have always been someone who is full of energy, but in those early days I found that at about 3pm in the afternoon I couldn't keep my eyes open. I was in the office by myself so I would just lock the office door and literally sleep for about two hours. It was a serviced office so reception would take all my calls. I would then wake up refreshed and carry on working but I kept giving myself a good talking to; where was my drive, my motivation? Why did I keep falling asleep?

My husband became more and more concerned when I would just fall asleep at home and he found it difficult to wake me up. This coincided with the cleaner at work trying to get into my office to clean it. She tried her key but couldn't get in because I was asleep on a blanket behind the door. She ran downstairs, convinced that I was dead, until the manager of the centre said, "Oh no, it's just Olive, she always has a nap around this time." I knew that something must be wrong with me and finally made an appointment to see my doctor. My blood test revealed a very low blood count and the doctor said he was surprised that I could actually stand up! I was immediately put on iron tablets and reviewed my diet to ensure that it was full of iron-rich foods.

A full medical examination revealed the need for me to have an operation and take sick leave for six weeks. Fortunately, my children were now teenagers and my husband was home, so they would be fine, but I panicked about the business. These were the crucial early days of building my reputation. The only person I could trust at this delicate time was my family, so my sister stepped in to help. We had phone calls and meetings but considering she knew nothing about my industry she did a fine job. I was back at my desk within four weeks and my husband drove me into the city and picked me up again each evening. It was sooner than recommended but sometimes you just have to get on with it. I never shared this with my clients; I kept smiling and cheerful throughout the experience.

My philosophy in life is, "Smile and the world smiles with you, cry and you cry alone." Clients do not call you to hear about your problems, they call so you can alleviate their concerns. So when they ask how I am I say, "I am fine thanks, how are you keeping?"

One lesson I learned from this experience is that you are what you eat. I had always eaten whatever I fancied, not for health, but by eating the iron-rich food I noticed a significant improvement in my health. I now keep healthy by a mixture of portion control and exercise and in August 2018, in preparation for attending my investiture at the palace in February 2019, I joined the David Lloyd gym near the Trafford Centre in Manchester. I booked the services of a personal trainer, the lovely Helena Brown, and as my husband was working away and I was living alone, I had my food delivered in calorie-controlled portions. Due to this three-pronged attack I lost a stone immediately and have continued to lose weight and tone up!

Ten years ago, I was sitting in the garden with my family, enjoying a barbecue and a few glasses of wine. My son, who regularly jogs and works out and was at the peak of his fitness, produced a skipping rope and started skipping, and seeing him doing it so effortlessly reminded me of my younger days. I asked him to hand me the skipping ropes so that I could demonstrate my own prowess at skipping.

It was such a liberating feeling! I leapt up in the air, enjoying the look of incredulity from my family - they never knew mum was so good at skipping! As I came down for the last time, I heard a sound like an elastic band snapping and my ankle collapsed. I couldn't move my foot and the pain was excruciating. My husband and son helped me into the car and drove me to the local hospital. I had ruptured my Achilles tendon and had to be in plaster for twelve weeks.

My diary was fully booked for the next few weeks so I called all my clients and informed them about my accident, assuring them that apart from my leg everything else was in perfect working order and I could still deliver training. For the local work I contacted a taxi company and arranged a contract with them, and they came with a van and transported me wherever I needed to go. I had a pair of crutches and a wheelchair for longer journeys. For a five-day programme I was to deliver in London, my husband took some time off and came with me.

For the next twelve weeks I continued working. I'd put my good leg on a chair, rested my leg in plaster to one side, remain upright and put a lot of passion into my presentation to keep everyone engaged. The story about how I ruptured my Achilles tendon was a great ice breaker!

Being in a wheelchair gave me some insight into how many restaurants and buildings are not wheelchair friendly. As a couple, my husband and I often go out for a meal together or with friends, and this was not always possible with my wheelchair. I also learned about the attitudes of some people who think that because you are in a wheelchair you have lost the power of speech! I remember sitting in the wheelchair beside my husband when someone stopped and asked my husband for directions. The man then asked him, "What's wrong with her?" looking at him and indicating me with his head. I remember shouting, "I am in a wheelchair, but I can speak!"

Suffice to say, if I ever hold skipping ropes in my hand now, the whole family shriek "NO!"

The Power of Music

In an article in *Psychology Today,* by Graham Collier, posted 3rd April 2012, he discusses the evocative power of music. He says that music comes in two forms. There are the impassioned responses that call for action of some sort, or there is music capable of working solely to induce a state of personal serenity. Music is a very important part of my life and if I feel down it can lift me to new heights. It can be any kind of music from Bob Marley to Pavarotti, Dolly Parton to Kiri Te Kanawa, George Benson to Roy Orbison. It can bring tears to my eyes, make me get up and dance, or just lie down and absorb it. When I facilitate training sessions, I always have music to set the scene and I often receive positive feedback about how hearing the music made people relax and enjoy the whole experience. I use music to keep me upbeat and happy, to create a joyful atmosphere.

The Power of Colour

I am not a gardener, but I appreciate the beauty of nature. When I travel abroad, I try to get up on a hill so that I can look down and admire the vista, casting my eyes over mountains, green rolling hills, beautiful flowers, the sea or a lake. I could sit there for hours just drinking it all in. The beauty of nature always has the power to lift my mood and bring me a sense of peace and tranquillity. As a child I used to go on school trips to the Lake District where we stayed in Ambleside, a beautiful part of the world with spectacular scenery, and I have many happy memories of those times.

When it comes to work, if I have an important meeting or a stressful day, I will wear something bold with a colour that lifts me up. I love reds, burnt orange, pinks etc. If it makes me feel good, I will wear it and walk into the room head held high feeling fabulous! Your use of colour as a professional can reflect your brand but also make you distinctive and memorable.

Mantras

I believe in the power of words, and I have mantras and poems that have deep meaning for me. A personal mantra is an affirmation to motivate and inspire you to be your best self. It is a positive phrase or statement that you use to affirm the way you want to live your life.

My very first mantra is something my Mum always says, "When life gets hard, just put one foot in front of the other." In other words, keep going. I have had to repeat this to myself many times, during my years in business.

Eleanor Roosevelt said, "No one can make you feel inferior without your consent." I play this one in my head, when I walk into a room and I feel like I don't belong.

And when I feel like giving up, I remember this quote by Michelle Obama, "Whether you come from a council estate or a country estate, your success will be determined by your own confidence and fortitude."

I have a tendency to try to do too many things at once so often need to put all my energies into one thing in order to glean the best results, so this mantra by Anthony Robbins reminds me to do this: "Where focus goes, energy flows."

I also have two pieces that resonate with me on many levels and just sitting down in a quiet space and reading them gives me strength and reasserts my power.

And Still I Rise – by Maya Angelou

Just like moons and like suns,
With the certainty of tides,
Just like hopes springing high,
Still I rise.

Our deepest fear is not that we are inadequate.
Our deepest fear is that we are powerful beyond measure.
It is our light, not our darkness that most frightens us.
We ask ourselves, who am I to be brilliant, gorgeous,
talented, fabulous?
Actually, who are you not to be? You are a child of god.
Your playing small does not serve the world.
There is nothing enlightened about shrinking,
So that others won't feel insecure around you.

Health and Wellbeing during the Covid 19 Pandemic

I returned from working in Curaçao as a keynote speaker for the Inspirational Ladies of the Caribbean event. I had thoroughly enjoyed the occasion, some great networking, and my stay at the Marriott Hotel, but had also found some time to explore this beautiful island. I arrived back in Manchester ready to pack my case, as I was soon to fly out to America to deliver some management development training for Brand Addition in St. Louis, when Jo Chapman, the HR Director, called me to discuss whether we should go ahead with the training. A few days later President Trump took the decision away from us when he banned travel to the USA from certain countries due to Covid-19, and we had no choice but to postpone the training. My bookings with three other organizations for face-to-face training both in the UK and abroad were also postponed. So apart from my coaching clients who were happy to use Facetime or Zoom, I had three months of work cancelled.

As the pandemic spread and we became aware of how serious and far-reaching Covid-19 was, the full enormity of its impact on our everyday life became clear. At the time, my husband was working in Ireland and both my children have their own homes and families, which meant that I was in lockdown alone.

My son and his partner would bring me some lovely dinners and leave them on the step, as we had to socially distance.

My daughter and her husband live in Wolverhampton, but they called me frequently to make sure that I was ok. I am not someone who enjoys being locked in the house on my own, although I have some friends who say they love it! Within two weeks my husband was able to return from Ireland, so I had some company at last.

Initially I saw this as a short-term glitch which would soon be over. However, as the true horror of Covid-19 unfolded I realised that there was no fixed time or date in the future when we could say categorically it would be at an end. I have worked in Manchester for over thirty years and have experienced many crises, both nationally and internationally. There were many frightening moments during the IRA bombings in Manchester on 15th June 1996, when we had to stay in our offices whilst we heard explosions and were gradually led out of our office by policemen and instructed to get out of the city centre. I remember six of us squashing into someone's car, we were so scared and just wanted to get home. During the London tube bombings, three members of my family were in London and it made me extremely anxious. Then there was the horror of 9/11, and the 2008 global recession. However, experiencing and working through all these events does help you to become resilient and develop various coping strategies. There are things you can control and things you cannot, you must start with yourself.

During the global recession I knew that it didn't impact on certain areas and countries, so my solution was to seek out organizations in those countries in order to sell them my services. I was also totally flexible regarding travel and was happy to work anywhere in the world. With Covid-19 the whole world was impacted by it, not only individuals but businesses, and because so many people lost their lives it seemed wrong to even think about business, there were much more serious issues at stake.

I wasn't used to the isolation, so I wasn't working to full capacity and I had a lot of time to think. I experienced many emotions. Initially I was impatient - when would this be over?! I could no longer see my family, children or grandchildren, or my friends, and I did have moments of despair. I had a lot of time for introspection, I realised that my whole life and work was spent with people.

Prior to the pandemic I had joined David Lloyd Health Club and had engaged the services of a personal trainer, attending classes three or four times per week. I had started to see results and was receiving compliments from my friends and clients regarding my weight loss. I had also made some new friends and become part of the social fabric of the gym, so I was devastated when it had to close because of the virus and imagined myself emerging from the house three months later, so huge that I would have difficulty getting out of the front door! I knew that I could not give in to this negative feeling and started to put together a plan that would see me through this situation.

I am married to an introvert who did not see any difference to his working day during lockdown. He has worked remotely previously and had no problem continuing to do so. I realised that I could not rely on just my husband to entertain me and I discussed this with my friends, some of whom were in lockdown alone. I subsequently became part of three Zoom meetings, two with sets of friends and another with my gym buddies. This proved a lifesaver during the long days when I just needed some good girly fun.

I was also forced to let go of my love of face-to-face contact and make use of other tools available to mentor, coach and train clients. I delivered a management development programme for seventeen people using Zoom. I used Microsoft Teams for coaching and delivered a webinar using WebEx. This is not my favourite form of communication, but this is the way the learning and development industry is going and I have to embrace it, or be left behind.

I recently listened to a webinar from the CIPD about the future of learning and development.

The guest speakers were from the BBC and accountancy firm PwC, and they were discussing the changes that had to be made to staff development during what they called "lockdown learning". One key message that emerged was that technology is at the heart of overcoming the pandemic and I realised that I needed to hone my skills and become an expert on the different platforms used for learning and development.

With regards to my physical wellbeing during the pandemic, I have discovered some beautiful walks around the area that I live in. Connecting with nature, "The Biophilia Hypothesis", is about humans' instinctive love of nature. On days when I felt claustrophobic, I would go for long walks and just seeing the beauty of nature around me lifted my spirits. I also have something called MyZone, an electronic device that you wear whilst exercising which connects to your phone and tells you how many calories you have burned during your workout. When the gym closed, they continued to keep in contact via various Apps. They set up a league table for gym members and each day you could see how you compared to your other connections. I am extremely competitive so this drives me to work harder and walk faster and further so that I can keep at the top of the league table. A positive outcome of all this exercise is that I did not gain weight and I slept better.

With this focus on self-care and looking after my physical and mental health, I know I will emerge from the Covid-19 lockdown stronger.

CHAPTER 17

LESSONS LEARNED

When I speak at conferences one of the questions always posed by the audience is about sharing the lessons that I have learned as a professional businesswoman. So here are my lessons!

(1) Understand your strengths and weaknesses; play to your strengths and find others who can fill the gaps. When I first opened my business, I handled the client-facing work and sales but quickly recruited an accountant and an IT specialist.

(2) Some new business owners believe that just by opening their business customers will flock to them. This will not happen. You need to build your brand and use the best means possible to build awareness of your business, whether it is designing a website, using social media, YouTube, etc. Constantly be aware of your potential audience and how you can attract them.

(3) Be persistent and tenacious. I rang the Manchester Evening News approximately ten times because I felt that I had an interesting story to tell. I was one of the first female Black training consultants in Manchester and I pushed my unique selling points. After much persistence, the newspaper sent a reporter to my office and printed my picture in the paper along with a write up about my new business venture. Believe in yourself, you can't give up, be tenacious, keep going.

(4) Don't be risk averse! About ten years ago an email popped into my Inbox, asking me to send a proposal for a management training programme for approximately fifty managers based in the Middle East. I wanted this piece of work; I love travelling and wanted to work globally. I contacted the client and discussed their requirements, and from our discussion I surmised that it would be beneficial to meet this client in person. I purchased a ticket to Egypt and arranged a meeting. I won the contract and it has had a far-reaching, long-lasting favourable impact on my business. From this initial opportunity I ended up working in over twenty countries.

(5) Be resilient. Over the past twenty years I have navigated my business through a major recession and more recently the Covid-19 pandemic. The most challenging parts were having to make staff redundant and searching for new markets for my business. I had to remain curious, learn new skills, seek new opportunities, and exploit them. I stayed optimistic and motivated, kept my energy levels up and believed in myself. It was difficult but I am stronger for it!

(6) Identify and exploit your key differentiator. We are all individuals and have something that makes us stand out from others. Mine is that I have a real passion for developing others, helping them to achieve their full potential whether an individual or an organization. I like to plan, deliver, and achieve. You could say it's my talent!

(7) Be credible. I made the decision to change my career from recruitment to Learning and Development/HR in 1998, and went on to gain a Post Graduate Diploma in Human Resource Management and a Masters degree in Human Resource Management. I am an Ambassador for Women of the Year award and a Northern Power Woman.

(8) Volunteer your services. This benefits you and others. When I opened my business in 1998, I felt very lonely, so I joined my local branch of the CIPD. This was the beginning of twenty years of volunteering, culminating in me becoming the Branch Chair in Manchester. I am also an Export Champion for the DIT and a mentor on the Entrepreneurial Accelerator for the NatWest.

(9) Make sure you have a social media presence. This is the only way to keep your brand current and relevant. I have delivered a webinar and taken part in an 'ignite' session (an ignite talk is a series of events where the speaker has five minutes to talk on a subject, accompanied by twenty slides, for fifteen seconds per slide) at the CIPD conference in Manchester. I also regularly post on Facebook, LinkedIn, Twitter, and Instagram. I have videos on YouTube and have taken part in a podcast which has helped keep my clients abreast of any developments, as well as encouraging new clients to contact me.

(10) Cherish your clients. Treat them with tender loving care. My clients know that I will work tirelessly to meet their requirements as their success is my success. Over the years their support and concern for me is what has allowed me to sustain my business.

(11) Have a close group of friends or contacts who you can call on. It is all about give and take, it is important to have people who can rely on and who can rely on you. Always be prepared to put yourself out for them if necessary.

CHAPTER 18

TESTIMONIALS AND RECOMMENDATIONS

Testimonials are written or recorded statements that support your credibility and level of expertise. They also strengthen your reputation by expressing the trust that other people have in you and your business. They also help to build your confidence and self-esteem.

Building Confidence and Self Esteem

I was not always the confident person that I am today, I gained professional confidence when I worked in recruitment and realised that I had a talent for being able to probe and draw out salient information from candidates looking for work. This meant that I was able to find them the type of job they desired. I discovered I had a flair for building rapport with clients, discussing their business needs and pinpointing their exact requirements, and ultimately I was good at matching the right member of staff to the right organization, thus meeting both their needs.

Gradually I built a good reputation in the recruitment industry. Many people would come to me to help them find employment more than once in their career as they wanted to progress to the next step. I had built trust with many organizations that would come to me for their staff requirements. When a new client joined the agency they would complete a form asking them how they had heard about us, and often they would tick the box that said 'recommendation' and would say things like, "You found my friend/work colleague/aunty a job". This was a light bulb moment for me; selling was good, but recommendations were even better.

The training consultancy market has always been extremely competitive, and I knew I had to work hard not just to gain business but to ensure that I delivered what the client needed to a high standard.

Some of the pieces of work I gained when I started my own business were because of my background in recruitment. I have also worked with an organization to help employees who were being made redundant prepare for interviews, develop their CV's and hone their interview techniques.

My contracts have included training on customer services and sales skills, and once again my recruitment experience meant my clients were confident that I had the necessary skills. As clients saw the positive impact of my training and the tangible benefits to the organization, I received more work. One of the keys to a successful outcome is clarifying with your client how they are going to evaluate and measure success. When you have completed the project and the client has given you positive feedback, it is a good time to request a written testimonial.

In 1998 we didn't have LinkedIn and clients would have the testimonial typed on their letterhead. As my collection of testimonials grew, I would bring a testimonial that either was from a similar industry to the prospective client or was for a similar training programme that the client had requested.

When a client is happy to commit to paper a recommendation for your services, this increases your self-confidence. They didn't have to choose you; they selected you and paid for your services, sometimes on more than one occasion. Proof that you are good at what you do!

With the advent of social media there is the opportunity to publicise your recommendations and LinkedIn is great for this. It is also important to keep your profile on LinkedIn fresh and up to date as it is where potential clients will do some research about you before contacting you. I have gained many pieces of work from LinkedIn.

No matter how good you are or knowledgeable about your industry, not every client will want to give you a glowing reference.

Some contracts will be for only a few days, some will be months or years. There has to be a connection with that client, where you are able to demonstrate understanding of their business and be able to bring your expertise to bear and add value.

Building and Maintaining Client Relationships

To gain a client's respect you have to demonstrate some key skills, for example, strategic thinking, the ability to analyse and use information and to have a professional and performance-orientated mindset. Then, as you build the relationship, personality comes into it. I have spent many hours around the board room where we discuss the business needs, but also had fun and laughter. I feel privileged when clients bring me fully into their business, examining all aspects from growth projections, financial constraints, and future plans. I see clearly where I fit in and work hard to play my part in achieving their goals and ultimately be successful. I give my all to the project and am extremely committed. My clients also see me as a part of their business.

I had been working with Packaging Automation in Knutsford for three years when they were shortlisted for the E3 Business Award held at the Macron Stadium in Bolton. They asked me to join them at their table at the award ceremony because I was part of their journey to success. When they were announced as the winners of the Manufacturing Business of the Year award, I was invited to join them on stage with the rest of the Directors. I was so proud and overwhelmed to be there with them. At one point I forgot that I was their guest and nearly went to the front to receive the award on their behalf!

On another occasion, I was working with Campanile Hotels and had trained staff at various locations on a programme called 'Stepping Forward', which had been very successful. They were holding an award ceremony for the staff and invited me along. Having trained the staff to then witness them receiving their awards was an amazing feeling.

I worked for Irwell Valley Housing for many years and the CEO at the time was Tom Manion, who unfortunately is no longer with us. Tom was a very unconventional CEO who had his own unique style, he was often dressed in jeans, jacket and white T shirt, and sometimes had a guitar in his hand. He was a published author and had his own band.

He believed in the power of music and singing was something his staff were used to. I was asked to speak at a staff meeting held at the Zion Centre in Manchester. After I delivered my speech, Tom got the guitar out and started to sing and he asked me and three other staff to sing backing vocals! I don't have the best voice in the world but am always happy to join in! I have some kind and thoughtful clients who understand the authentic me and like me for who I am.

It is great to work with clients who like and accept you, and you in turn like and respect them. This makes for a mutually beneficial long-term relationship.

Collaboration with Clients

Over the years I have always looked for opportunities to collaborate with my clients, for instance inviting them to events and nominating them for any suitable awards where appropriate, having joint events, interviewing them for YouTube videos, etc. Many of my clients become friends and this friendship is often maintained after we stop working together. I also enjoy reading about my clients' successes. For marketing purposes, we have a newsletter in which we have "client of the month", where the client has the opportunity to share the story of their job role and the history of their organization. They also share details of how they have worked with my company and some of the projects we have worked on (see Appendix).

CHAPTER 19

THE NEXT STEP

Looking to the future, we made a decision to offer our training programmes to our clients online, via the "OSR Virtual Leadership Academy" on our website, and which consists of a suite of leadership programmes for global leaders, delivered virtually. These include the benefits of virtual learning, i.e. it is convenient, flexible, reduces your carbon footprint, has measurable results and is cost effective. Our first course is, "Leading for impact in the 2020s", covering leadership styles, communication, high performance, and change management.

We had just launched this when the Covid-19 pandemic happened, which made our online course even more relevant. During the months of April, May and June we continued to offer leadership development programmes by using platforms such as Zoom, Microsoft Teams and WebEx.

More recently we have invested in property in the Caribbean and established some strategic alliances, with a view to creating and offering clients leadership retreats based on various Caribbean Islands.

I will continue to offer consultancy, facilitation and speaking engagements and executive coaching, as well as working with organizations on their diversity and inclusion strategy, and with female entrepreneurs to help them develop their skills and achieve their goals. Clients will be able to access my services from OSR in the UK or my offices in Dominica, West Indies, via my website or my social media channels.

CHAPTER 20

CONCLUSION

I started writing this book at the beginning of March 2020, just as the Covid-19 virus started to spread around the world and began to impact on my life. Prior to Covid-19 I would never have spent three months without some form of face-to-face interaction with my friends, family and clients, and so the time spent in enforced isolation has given me space to reflect on my life, and work on my book. I am fortunate that I have had this positive experience, however, the changes to my life and the limitations the Covid-19 pandemic imposed on us all have been extremely difficult, and speaking to neighbours and friends about the challenges of living through the pandemic is a shared experience that we can all relate to.

Reflecting on the past twenty-two years since opening OSR, I have been remembering the challenges and how I overcame them, and realise that whenever I was in the midst of a difficult situation it felt like it was going to last forever and I would never get over it. The fact is that I did get over it, and each time I rose like a phoenix from the ashes, stronger and more determined than before. In spite of all the negativity at the moment I refuse to be bowed or cowed by it; I am looking to the horizon and visualising a positive outcome. One day we will look back on this time and realise that the coping strategies we used to survive have become weapons in our armoury, making us stronger and more resilient.

My hope is that this book inspires others to aim high and achieve their goals and I would like to leave you with two lines from Nelson Mandela's favourite poem.

I am the master of my fate:
I am the captain of my soul.
From Invictus by William Ernest Henley

APPENDIX

CLIENT RECOMMENDATIONS

The following are extracts from the OSR newsletter and LinkedIn.

Sam Ashton
Commercial Director of Packaging Automation Ltd, contributed to our newsletter:

"April is usually the time of year when Performance Management appraisals are looming on the horizon for many organizations, however, at Packaging Automation Ltd (PA), a Global Engineering and Manufacturing Company based in the heart of Cheshire, this year they are fully equipped with the tools and techniques to maximise employee engagement.

At PA the leadership and management teams, along with the employees, have undertaken a bespoke training programme delivered by Olive Strachan Resources that has enabled the organization to understand the critical factors that influence both employee engagement and disengagement. The OSR delivery helped them to identify and address gaps in employee engagement across the team and aided them to go on and develop high trust relationships within and across the PA workforce.

Established 51 years ago in Wilmslow by the Grandfather, Arthur Penn, the family run business has grown from strength to strength. Based on the sturdy foundations of integrity and vision PA are passionate about every aspect of their business and the 'people' are the lifeblood of the organization. Customers are key and their clients include many 'Blue Chip' organizations. Although PA have agents who operate in Europe, Turkey, Dubai, and Australia, they are proud to have their roots in Great Britain and they are truly 'Engineered in England'. The company USP is based upon responsiveness, versatility, communication, and passion.

A trained Engineer and Accountant, PA's Commercial Director, Sam Ashton, who is the granddaughter of founder Arthur Penn, is delighted with the implementation of the new appraisal reviews and staff handbook designed and prepared by Olive Strachan."

Sam's comments:

"The effect the OSR Employee Engagement programme has had on all the staff is truly rewarding and promising for the future. 'The culture change is evident, and everyone is more motivated, it has been an enriching experience for everyone involved."

The OSR programme had to fit within the company's 'Orbit' which is a long-term planning tool PA use under the guidance of the 'Growth Accelerator' initiative. Employee Engagement was one of the Orbit goals and Continuous Improvement was another.

"As part of the OSR Programme, Olive interviewed a selection of staff before designing the programme and spent many days providing in depth training with the management teams and team leaders as well as every employee. She helped to motivate, presented opportunities and changed the perception of Appraisals within the workforce."

Sam goes on to say:

"Olive Strachan is a hidden gem. She is vibrant, engaging and energetic in everything she does, and her positivity radiates and influences everyone."

Anyone who needs help or advice with Employee Engagement needs Olive Strachan as she can add value to any organization. The change in our employees' performance has increased by over 95% since we adopted OSR's systems and procedures. I have no hesitation in recommending Olive and OSR if anyone requires support with their Appraisal systems."

Client of the Month!

Introducing my client of the month! I've recently been working with BioBank and helping them enhance the already brilliant work they do!

Who are you/your business?

Gail Cross, Head of HR. I've worked at UK Biobank for four years now and when I joined, we did not have an HR department and only a small workforce. We have now tripled the size of our workforce and have a robust HR department which have rolled out a number of employee benefits, best practice HR processes and systems and created a more engaged workforce. The focus of the HR department is always to ensure that the work we implement brings value to both the people, develops a continuous improvement culture, and strives to maintain a motivated workforce.

UK Biobank is a major national health resource set up with the aim of improving the prevention, diagnosis and treatment of a wide range of serious and life-threatening illnesses. Between 2006 and 2010, UK Biobank recruited over 500,000 volunteers from across the country to take part. All donated biological samples for future analysis, provided detailed information about themselves, and agreed to have their health followed. Enhancement projects are now underway to add further value to this valuable research resource.

UK Biobank was established with the backing of a number of major funding bodies and is a registered charity. Whilst we are physically headquartered in Cheadle, direction and strategy take input from senior academics and other experts from across the UK and around the world.

How have you found working with Olive?

Olive has a bubbly, infectious personality that you can't help engaging with and respond positively to her. Olive's natural style enables all types of delegates to interact with her training courses.

Olive has a bank of HR knowledge and experience that enables her to adapt her style to a wide range of audiences and to be able to bring the training to life with work related experiences that others can relate to. Olive has the ability to make her events light-hearted, whilst maintaining professionalism and addressing the purpose of the course.

Has working together with OSR helped your business?

OSR helped me to design a bespoke equality and diversity course to enhance our employees' knowledge in this area. This was felt important for the organization due to the diverse range of staff who work at UK Biobank from 13 different countries. The course has identified a number of key areas we wish to work on, that without our employees attending this training we may not have become aware of. I'm sure we will continue working with Olive on future projects.

What can we look forward to from UK BioBank?

We will be looking at creating an international day at work to further develop greater understanding of different cultures and ways of working. We will also be looking at making our values more visible and easier to understand in all areas of the business as a result of the equality and diversity training Olive delivered for us.

Client of the Month!

Larisa Halilovic, who is currently the Education and Professional Development Consultant, Director of an International Cultural Relations Organization in Bosnia and Herzegovina.

What support have you received from OSR/Olive?
I have had the pleasure of working with Olive at different stages of my career and in different settings. Early on, as a participant on Olive's training sessions, I was able to further develop my assertiveness and management skills and Olive was superb at bringing out my leadership potential.

How has working with Olive helped you?
Subsequently, on several occasions, Olive worked with my team locally and regionally as a trainer and helped us improve our soft skills and team cohesion.

Needless to say, Olive's tips and tricks are still very much in use and passed onto our growing team.

What would you say to anyone thinking of booking OSR?

Olive was also one of our keynote speakers representing the UK at an international HR conference in Sarajevo. Her amazing energy, practical advice and inspiring stories got the audience fully engaged and with lots to think about and work on in their own workplace.

What's next for you?

Working with Olive has deeply affected my personal career path and her intervention helped me place focus on my strengths and identify areas which need further development. Currently as a senior consultant, trainer and a director of an international organization, I can comfortably say that working with Olive can help both executives and early career professionals individually, as well as any teams wishing to grow and excel.

LinkedIn recommendation:

Ono Okeregha, Director at Immigration Advice Service, July 24, 2019

My business was looking for a consultant to provide coaching and training to our management team and we went through a process of interviewing various consultants, but as soon as Olive walked through the door we knew she was the right person for us and we have never looked back. The first thing you will notice immediately about Olive is her energy, her infectious, vivacious personality and charisma which she uses effectively to deliver her coaching and training. She has huge knowledge and experience in leadership development, performance appraisal and improvement and her work with us has had a positive impact on the skills and knowledge of our management team and growth in the business. I would recommend Olive to anyone looking to inject energy and dynamism into their business whilst acquiring the necessary skills to improve and grow.

ACKNOWLEDGEMENTS

To my wonderful family, Errol, Rhia and Ricky, you have been part of the OSR story from day one to the present day; I value your input and support. I am blessed to have you all in my life, together we have achieved great things!

To my friend Madeleine Mitchell Rishton, thank you for holding my hand through the process of writing and publishing my book. Your advice to "speak with my own authentic voice" and to believe in my abilities was just what I needed. Having a published author of three books as my mentor gave me confidence; your knowledge and expertise was invaluable.

To my friend Candace Edwards, who I rang and asked for help; we didn't let the fact that you now live in Spain stand in our way! Thank you for putting up with my constant WhatsApp calls. You have done an amazing job in editing and proofreading my book, your genuine interest, dedication and professionalism played a key part in the finished product.

To Ruth Robinson from Brighter Business, Ruth and her team have been responsible for the PR and Marketing for OSR for the past two years; I could not think of anyone I would rather work with to ensure that my book receives the right kind of exposure.

To Mark Cattell of MAWebdesign Ltd, with whom I have worked for over a year, for designing the front cover of my book. Mark used his creativity to interpret my vision and bring it to reality.

To Nancy Jaeger, who was kind enough to read one of the first drafts of my book. Your critical feedback helped me to see the book through your eyes and to make appropriate amendments.

To my friend, Jules DeLuca, thank you for reading my book as a critical friend, giving me the benefit of your ideas, wisdom and friendship.

Thank you to David Fenton, the only male to read my book so far. I really appreciate the ideas you shared, which I implemented. It is great to get insight from a male viewpoint.

ABOUT OLIVE

Global business woman, entrepreneur and founder of Olive Strachan Resources, ex-Chair of CIPD and CIPD Fellow, Olive has spent over twenty years developing managers and leaders across the world.

Awarded an MBE in 2019, named as a Northern Power Woman in 2020 @IamNPW and an Ambassador for Women of the Year 2020, Olive is also Head Judge for the IoD NW Director of the Year Award 2020

SPEAKER: Guest Speaker | Conference Presenter | Diversity & Inclusion Speaker

COACH: 1:1 executive and management coaching for business and personal growth, helping you gain motivation, confidence, perspective and work life balance.

CONSULTANT: Design & deliver bespoke programmes on leadership development, performance appraisal and change management.

TRAINER: Expert leadership & management trainer delivering innovative training to develop effective business leaders.

NON EXEC DIRECTOR: CIPD Chair | DiT Northern Powerhouse Export Champion Entrepreneurial Spark

SPECIALITIES: L&D | Leadership Development | SME Growth | Managing Performance | Performance Appraisal | Women in Business | Diversity & Inclusion

OLIVE STRACHAN RESOURCES

Olive Strachan MBE, Chartered FCIPD, MSc (HRM)
Management Development| Performance Improvement| Career Coaching |
Bringing you inspiring, engaging and passionate training, that delivers business benefits!

Contact Us:

Tel: +044 (0)161 509 2017 | Mob: 07739 763 750
Email: info@olivestrachan.com
www.olivestrachan.com

LinkedIn: https://www.linkedin.com/in/olivestrachan/
Facebook: https://www.facebook.com/OliveStrachanTraining/
Twitter: https://twitter.com/olivestrachan/
Instagram: https://www.instagram.com/olivestrachan/

Printed in Great Britain
by Amazon